THE FLASH OF LIGHTNING

By the same author:
My Father's Son
Kean
Singapore Goes Off The Air
The Heart of Fame
The Little Tour (with Constantine FitzGibbon)
The Offenders (with Derrick Sington)
Crime, Punishment and Cure (with Derrick Sington)
The Prodigy
Six Studies in Hypocrisy
Crime in our Century
The Punitive Obsession

The Flash of Lightning

A Portrait of Edmund Kean

GILES PLAYFAIR

WILLIAM KIMBER · LONDON

First published in 1983 by
WILLIAM KIMBER & CO. LIMITED
100 Jermyn Street,
London, SW1Y 6EE

© Giles Playfair, 1983
ISBN 0-7183-0399-7

Typeset by Jubal Multiwrite Limited
Printed and bound in Great Britain by
Biddles Ltd, Guildford and King's Lynn

For Lee, Piers and Sanchia

Contents

List of Illustrations

Foreword

I suspect that Edmund Kean was the greatest actor who ever lived. He was undoubtedly the most exciting. When he died in 1833 no one would have believed that this physical wreck of a man was only in his forties — in the prime of life.

Willson Disher says in the *Oxford Companion to the Theatre* (1950) that 'biographers who whitewash Kean must surely miss the clue to his art and his character. His spirit was untamably wild. Unpublished diaries by Winston, Elliston's house-manager at Drury Lane, give a day-to-day account of uncouth exploits.' I don't believe that in my earlier biography* of him I tried (or wished) to whitewash Kean, but I did feel a certain empathy with him — of the kind which made him my hero and obliged me to call him Edmund rather than Kean. The unpublished diaries have since been published (1974) by the Society for Theatre Research.† They have also been used as the centrepiece of a recent biography by Raymund FitzSimons.**

Now that I have been given the opportunity to write this present work with Winston's diaries available to me, I may say right away that they — I deal with them in detail in their proper place — have neither deepened nor altered my understanding of Kean. To begin with, they cover only a comparatively brief period of his career, from 1819 to 1827, and for two years of that time he was in America. Secondly I was already aware he drank too much, that he was obsessively fearful of rival

---

*   *Kean*, Geoffrey Bles, 1939, and Reinhardt and Evans, 1950.
†   *A Drury Lane Journal* Selections from James Winston's diaries 1819–1827, edited by Alfred L. Nelson and Gilbert B. Cross.
** *Edmund Kean: Fire from Heaven*, Hamish Hamilton, 1976.

actors, that he suffered from venereal disease and that he consorted with whores. The same could be said of other actors. The diaries merely add some salacious details to this category of weaknesses, and even so sometimes give an exaggerated or unfair impression. For instance, the entry for 15th March, 1823 reads, 'Kean this evening at the theatre very drunk indeed.' That would suggest that Kean acted when he was very drunk. But in fact, though he doubtless came to the theatre very drunk, he wasn't due to give a performance until 17th March. Which would have given him ample time to sober up!

Thirdly, many of the entries that concern Kean are hearsay, and cannot, therefore, be accepted as true. In other words they are not what Winston has observed for himself, but what has been told him by a third person or, quite likely, boastfully or jokingly, by Kean himself.

I am ready to accept FitzSimons' deduction that Winston hated actors, and Kean in particular, but just the same it seems to me that he has read more into the diaries than can be justified. The entry for 17th January, 1820, reads:

> Kean requested the rehearsal might not be till twelve as he should get drunk that night — said he had frequently three women to stroke during performances and that two waited while the other was served. Penley said he had [formerly] seen Storace waiting for her turn. This night he had one woman (Smith)* though he was much infected.

Mr FitzSimons says that Kean 'shocked' Winston by telling him this, but there is nothing in Winston's relation of it to show that he was more shocked than thrilled. On another occasion FitzSimons has Winston recording a detail with 'disgust', but, again, there is nothing to suggest he was more disgusted than overjoyed.

Part of an entry for 6th February, 1827 reads:

> Kean came to my house [and] said that the papers were abusing him for not acting a new part in Knowles' play . . .
> 'I have not refused to play in that play; but, as I play only

---

*   Drury Lane actress.

thirteen or fourteen nights at a time, I have enough characters.'
When I observed public men must make up their minds to
all sorts of attacks, he said [?], 'Ah, give me bread and
cheese and a couple of whores.'

Mr FitzSimons interprets that as an occasion when Kean arrived
at the 'theatre' 'drunk', when Winston 'lectured' him on the
'duty of the actor to his public', when Kean listened to Winston
'in astonishment' and when he finally said 'contemptuously'
"Give me bread and cheese and a couple of whores." Even
Willson Disher who, in an admittedly fictionalised biography
of Kean, had the use of Winston's diaries, did not go so far as
that. He wrote that Kean 'was sympathetically assured that
public men must expect such attacks'.

Apart from the diaries, to which both Willson Disher and
George Raymond, Elliston's biographer, had access, Mr Fitz-
Simons had no sources, so far as I'm aware, that had not been
available to previous biographers. I shall, as I have said, deal
with the diaries in detail later. But, while they may give an
excellent picture of backstage life at Drury Lane, they do not,
let me repeat, affect in any essential sense my view of Edmund
Kean.

PART ONE

The Painful Climb

1

No proof has yet been found of exactly when Kean was born, but according to what in my view is the best available evidence the date of his birth was certainly 17th March, and the year was very probably 1789. That was his birthday according to Miss Tidswell (or 'Aunt' Tid, as Kean called her) as recorded by Barry Cornwall, his first biographer whose book was published in 1835, although he himself did not accept it as correct. However, it is supported by a certain amount of independent evidence that I discovered, including details given on Kean's passport, and a couple of letters which Harold Hillebrand reproduced* and which were written by Kean as a very young man when he could have had no conceivable motive for lying about his age. The alternative date of 4th November, 1787 was introduced by his second biographer, F.W. Hawkins,† also on the alleged authority of Miss Tidswell, although she had been in her grave for some 23 years by the time his book was published in 1869. There is no independent evidence whatever to support it. But for some reason, which I cannot explain, it has been preferred by all subsequent biographers and encyclopaedists except me.

Kean was a bastard. He was born in an attic in Gray's Inn that had been loaned by George Saville Carey, the posthumous son of Henry Carey, composer of 'Sally in Our Alley' and arguably of 'God Save the King', to his wayward daughter Ann. Henry Carey committed suicide in the prime of life, and was found afterwards with only a halfpenny in his pocket. George Saville Carey inherited a modicum of his father's talent, and all

---

*   *Edmund Kean*, New York, Columbia University Press, 1933.
†   *Life of Edmund Kean*, London, 1869.

his improvidence. Ann Carey, or Nance Carey as she was known familiarly, inherited her father's vices but little or none of his mental equipment. She called herself, delicately enough, an itinerant actress and street hawker. Actually, she had the natural instincts, if not the commercial acumen, of an ordinary prostitute. She was an attractive wench, with a fine pair of dark eyes. But she made her appeal to the dissolute; and she got herself up to look precisely as virtuous as she was. Her gradual degeneration into a low, dissipated old woman was inevitable. Illegitimate children were the unfortunate consequence of her pleasure, and to these she eventually grew quite accustomed. There is no telling how many bastards were hers. But, as late as 1830, when she was three years from her grave, she still had a young boy in her charge.

Edmund's father was a mentally unbalanced surveyor's apprentice. He lived with his two brothers Moses and Aaron, and their widowed married sister, Mrs Price, at 9 Little St Martin's Lane. He died when Edmund was three, by throwing himself off the roof of his house. He was aged twenty-two, and left his son nothing except his name and his passion for brandy.

It is impossible to give anything approaching an ordered account of Edmund's childhood, since so much of it is buried in myth. But one may guess at the influences that helped to make him what he became. And chief among these was probably Charlotte Tidswell. She was reputedly the mistress of Moses Kean, Edmund's uncle, though she did not live in the same house as he did. Though only a small part actress at Drury Lane, whereas Moses was a well-known ventriloquist, she was several cuts above him in the social scale — or rather she had been. She never knew her mother, and she was brought up in luxurious circumstances by her father, an army officer, and sent over to France for her education. But her father, who lived extravagantly, died young and bankrupt. Charlotte found herself at the age of seventeen penniless, homeless and alone. It was then that she came under the protection of her first lover, 'Jockey', the ill-reputed eleventh Duke of Norfolk. He had the best of Charlotte's youth, and when she was twenty-three, instead of pensioning her off, he used his influence to obtain her an engagement to play small parts at Drury Lane theatre, where she had been ever since, earning £3.00 a week.

Moses' sister, Mrs Price, whom Edmund knew as 'Aunt' Price, suggested to Miss Tidswell that she should take the child to live with her after his mother had put him out to nurse, where he was ill-treated. That was around 1790. In December, 1792, Moses Kean died, and it is easy to understand how Charlotte must have found in the small child entrusted to her care consolation for the drabness and emptiness of her existence. She was determined that he should grow up with the instincts and qualities of her own early background. He would, of course, have to be an actor, for the stage was her only environment and would be his. She lived at 12 Tavistock Row, Covent Garden, within a few minutes walk of Drury Lane, and she had no influence, no connections even, outside the theatre. But at least she could teach Edmund to be an aristocrat in his profession. She had marked him out for great-ness and she would see to it that he became a great tragedian like Garrick, and unlike the ordinary run of vulgar, illiterate players, a cultured, polished and scholarly man.

As soon as Edmund was old enough, Charlotte (or 'Aunt' Tid as he was taught to call her) sent him to school; she also had him taught singing by Incledon and fencing by Angelo, who in their particular crafts were both masters at Drury Lane. Charlotte herself after ten years' experience had learned enough of the tricks of the trade to be a good tutor, and she gave Edmund his first groundings in the study of Shakespeare, encouraging him to feel as well as understand the lines he repeated after her and making him rehearse his speeches for hours on end in front of a mirror.

At the age of eight, Edmund was already something of a theatrical prodigy and had played several small parts at Drury Lane. But he was temperamentally a difficult child — in Charlotte's own words, 'active, forward, prone to mischief and neither to be led nor driven'. He had, too, already developed a considerable idea of his own importance. When Miss Tidswell took him with her to Drury Lane, he liked to go up to the Green Room because there, surrounded by a circle of senti-

mental old players, he would recite and declaim and be applauded and told what a clever little boy he was. But when he was
actually engaged at rehearsals and was just one among a whole
bunch of child actors he did not enjoy himself half so well.
Nor did he scruple to shirk school just as often as he felt inclined
to do so. Charlotte tried her best to teach him obedience, and
to prevent him leaving his bed at night time to lead the wild
life of a guttersnipe in the streets round Covent Garden. But
she was an unsubtle disciplinarian. Though she beat him, locked
him in his room, tied him to his bedpost and — more ingenious
— encircled his neck in a large dog collar, with her name and
address inscribed on it, she failed to break his spirit.

Edmund found the opportunity for new adventures, when
Nance Carey asked for her son's return. The probability is that
it was on his own insistence that he left to embark on a life in
which there was no sort of order, permanence or security.
Nance Carey, as he soon realised, simply wanted him for what
he could bring in. She made him run messages, she exhibited
his youthful histrionic talents and commandeered his earnings,
but in return she gave him nothing except an occasional beating;
no kindness, no praise, no disinterested instruction.

Nevertheless, his association with his mother helped to
develop his character. He learned what it was like to run around
loose, to be lonely and hungry and cold. He went with cheap
travelling companies to barns and stables and fair-grounds, and
became expert in the lowest tricks of his trade — tumbling,
clowning, riding a horse bareback — and learned in his rough
and ready way how to fend for himself.

Yet Charlotte's influence in his very early years — too soon
cut off — had left its indelible mark. Now he regarded 12
Tavistock Row as home, and would often return there for
brief intervals; not, it is true, in the spirit of the prodigal son,
but because he realized that Aunt Tid was the only one in the
world who really cared for him and on whose assistance he
could count. He did not know why he yearned so passionately
for success or why he was so aggressively determined to be
treated as a gentleman of consequence. But these yearnings,
alien both to his fortune and environment, were irrepressible.

One person at least noticed that he had qualities not usually found in a Thespian guttersnipe. She was a Mrs Clarke — a lady of means and position, rich enough to keep a butler and well connected enough to be blessed with at least a couple of titled relatives.

Nance Carey, in between her theatrical engagements, worked as a street hawker, and Mrs Clarke became one of her best customers, paying double the proper price for Marechale powder, Jessamine Pomatum, genuine Eau de Luce and occasionally presenting the dilapidated saleswoman with some of her own cast-off fineries.

She first set eyes on Edmund when he was acting as his mother's errand-boy. He looked half-starved, his clothes were wretchedly shabby and the hat which he carried in his diminutive hand was too tattered to be fit for outdoor wear. But Mrs Clarke felt more than pity for him, for he was, in spite of his poverty-stricken appearance, a strikingly beautiful child. His auburn hair was a rich mass of tangled curls; he had his father's handsome Jewish-looking features, and his eyes, though like his mother's, were even larger and more noticeably brilliant.

He had, too, an air about him which astonished and captivated Mrs Clarke, for it seemed touchingly inappropriate to his age and environment. Admittedly, his manners were a trifle theatrical (especially the way he bowed), but they were none the less graceful and courteous. He knew how to behave in a lady's house. Moreover, he was already very accomplished. He could act scenes from *Richard III* and *Hamlet*, and he could play the Clown and Harlequin into the bargain.

Mrs Clarke wanted this boy for her own, and she persuaded Ann Carey (in return, presumably, for a suitable remuneration) to give him up. She clothed him as a respectable little boy, sent him to school, and treated him occasionally to an evening at the play when the Kembles were performing. She gave him good food to eat and a comfortable bed to sleep in. The bed particularly appealed to his fancy. He called it his 'bed of roses' because of the floral design printed on the cotton curtains with which it was draped.

Edmund entertained Mrs Clarke and her friends with regular

displays of his histrionic powers. Nothing delighted him more than the chance to act alone in front of a grown-up audience. The excitements of transforming a section of Mrs Clarke's drawing room into Richard III's tent, of fastening a belt, with a real sword attached to it, round his small waist, of dressing his head in a large feathered riding hat and finally of performing scenes from his favourite play entirely by himself — all these were only excelled by gratification at the applause which greeted his efforts.

Edmund responded to the fuss Mrs Clarke made of him by behaving impeccably in her house. And that must have been for quite a while. But unfortunately his first lapse from grace was his last. It happened that a country gentleman with his wife and two small daughters came to stay. He, unlike Mrs Clarke and her town-bred friends, did not consider good manners and histrionic virtuosity atonement enough for social inferiority. At dinner while Edmund was amusing the two small daughters with animated details of the play they were all going to see, the country gentleman spoke his mind. 'What!' he exclaimed. 'Does *he* go with us in the boxes?'

Edmund jumped up from the table scarlet in the face. Mrs Clarke caught his hand as he passed and told him to get a seat in the pit. He shook his head, left the room and a few minutes later slammed out of the front door. For the next seven days he was missing.

A friendly ostler eventually brought him back to Mrs Clarke. Edmund's story was that he'd begged his way to Portsmouth with the idea of joining the navy. But his offers to become a sailor had merely met with repulses, rude treatment and beatings. So he had returned to London determined to die, a martyr to the insult from that 'unfeeling' country gentleman, as near to Mrs Clarke's home as possible.

Mrs Clarke could not really understand why he should have felt insulted nor why he should have repaid her manifold kindnesses so ill. After all, there was, in her view, little difference between his impulsive display of wounded pride and a sudden tendency on the part of a favourite dog to snap at strangers. As it was, she forgave him, tended him and restored him to physical health. But obviously she could keep him in her care no longer. He had proved too dangerously unruly. He needed a man to look after him.

The account of Edmund's association with Mrs Clarke is drawn from an unsigned manuscript belonging to the London Theatre Museum. One cannot be certain that it is true in every detail, but certainly Edmund's reaction as a child to what he termed an insult was characteristic of his behaviour as a man. Moreover, his reaction to Mrs Clarke's treatment of him shows that his spirit was not '*untamably* wild', Equally the fantasies of himself that he invented afterwards — that he spent three years at Eton College from 1803 to 1806 and that he was the illegitimate son of Miss Tidswell and the Duke of Norfolk — give a clue to what he was convinced was his due in respect from the world at large.

Again, one does not know how long Edmund remained under Mrs Clarke's care and attended school regularly. But it must have been for quite a considerable time, for by 1804, at the age of fifteen when he began his life as a strolling player, he was reasonably well-educated, and this in the days when two-thirds of the population could neither read nor write.

On 4th April, 1810, he sent a letter to Mrs Clarke that incidentally testified to his own belief that he was born on 17th March, 1789. In it, he told her of his marriage two years before, and expressed his undying gratitude for all she had done for him. In a second letter, dated 17th May, 1810, he wrote:

> To give you a description of Mrs Kean as she ever has and still continues to appear in my eyes is impossible. ... I soon led her to the altar, by which she made me the happiest of men.

He had married in 1808 when he was not yet twenty a woman nine years older than himself. At the time of his letters to Mrs Clarke his words about that event were already much braver than true.

2

The country was the only school of dramatic art. It was a harsh, merciless school, and yet very few who sought fame and fortune on the stage could avoid it. The plight of provincial or strolling players varied according to their status. Some acted in large, well-equipped Theatres Royal, others in playhouses of the smaller towns, others in barns and stables where grass had grown through derelict floorboards and where the air was rank with the smell of burnt oil. But one and all worked like navvies for managers who never rewarded them with more than a living wage and who quite frequently paid them less.

Edmund Kean was nine years in this school. And he suffered agonies, of mind at least, which in the history of the stage have no parallel. But those years not only perfected his art. They created it.

This is not to say that there was anything extraordinary about the hardships that he endured. The bare facts of his struggle for recognition could be told, with few variations, of almost any of his famous contemporaries, with the exception of Charles Mayne Young and William Charles Macready, both of whom were better born than he. They were to be among his foremost and most feared rivals. But in fact though Edmund fared worse than some, he fared a great deal better than many others of his cruelly precarious profession who hardly rose above their beginnings.

It is sadly revealing in the light of after-events that Edmund did not hate the stroller's life from the outset. He saw no reason to fear the future when on Easter Monday of 1804 he joined Mr Samuel Jerrold's company at Sheerness.

Samuel Jerrold, ancestor of so many Jerrolds distinguished in literature and on the stage, was by no means in the first flight of country managers. But his Sheerness theatre, fitted up with boxes, pit and gallery, was better equipped than the exalted barns and stables which served the drama in most of the small towns of the United Kingdom. And though it was surreptitiously used by smugglers for the secretion of casks of hollands, it was also patronised by playgoers. The Napoleonic war was having a good effect on theatrical business in Sheerness. The town was full of sailors, and nautical drama was particularly popular.

Edmund, dressed in boy's costume and still only fifteen, was engaged as the star performer at a salary of fifteen shillings a week. He opened as George Barnwell, and thereafter played the 'whole round of tragedy, opera, farce, interlude and pantomime'. He did not mind hard work if it gave him the opportunity to show off his versatility. And as for the salary, fifteen shillings was enough to live on and money was anyway a trifling consideration. Position was what mattered. Though he can hardly have hoped to go straight from Sheerness to Drury Lane as leading tragedian, he didn't doubt that he'd be there soon enough.

It was subordination that Edmund found intolerable, and he had his initial taste of that in the following year when he joined a company of players in Belfast. The Belfast theatre was a Theatre Royal and was directed by Michael Atkins, one of the best-known and most influential of provincial managers. Edmund might well have been proud to think that, still in his teens, he had got a job with Michael Atkins, and he might have concluded, as perhaps he did at first, that he had travelled a long way upwards since his Sheerness engagement only twelve months ago.

But he was no longer the petted prodigy, with the pick of the best parts in tragedy, comedy, interlude and pantomime. Instead, he was just a very junior member of a company of players in Belfast unnoticed by the manager and 'scarcely permitted to deliver a message'. He was a supernumerary ordered to play whatever walk-on parts happened to be going and shoved on to the stage in any old, faded costume that might be left over from the theatre wardrobe. For him there was no glory and no applause. He was simply a strolling player of whose existence the public was scarcely aware.

He hated being insignificant; it hurt his pride unreasonably, and it appeared to him that everyone was set on humiliating him. He became gloomy, morose and introspective. He roamed about by himself day-dreaming, wondering how he could make men realize that he was destined for greatness. He was a young man without much wit or intellect, and superficially he was very unattractive. He had no personal charm, no natural wit or *bonhomie*. Through shyness he avoided his fellow actors, and naturally they did not go out of their way to bother with him. So that with reason he imagined himself despised and deliberately ignored. Sometimes he went to the tavern, for he found that drink loosened his tongue and enabled him to be more self-assertive.

In August (1805), Mrs Siddons, the Queen of Tragedy, was specially engaged by Michael Atkins to play for a few nights at the Belfast Theatre Royal. Edmund, in the days of his fame, was to tell a completely fictitious story about this event. According to him, he was chosen to play the leading part of Osmyn to Mrs Siddons' Zara in *The Mourning Bride*, and appeared drunk on the stage so that he ruined the effect of the great actress's performance. Mrs Siddons was horrified to learn next evening that he was again chosen to play opposite her. At first, she refused to appear 'with that dreadful little man', but was at last persuaded to give him another chance. She did not regret her lenience, for on this occasion he acted so brilliantly that Mrs Siddons, generous in her praise of him, murmured at the end, 'You have played very well, Sir, very well. It's a pity — there's too little of you to do anything.'

That story, though a total fabrication, tells a lot about Edmund. One can imagine him so easily — an awkward, shy, diminutive figure — standing in the wings enviously watching Mrs Siddons' performance, thinking that it was really his right to be the hero to her heroine, imagining how he would outshine her and how he would leap at once into prominence. Most young actors, whatever the extent of their own fame in after years, would have remembered how magnificent Mrs Siddons was, how devotedly they had worshipped at her shrine, how timid they had been in her presence. Not so Edmund; he was always the hero of his own adventures, true or imagined.

Actually, according to Barry Cornwall, his first biographer,*

---

*   *Life of Edmund Kean*, London 1835.

there was good authority for believing that he did attract Mrs Siddons' attention, and, though he would never have admitted as much, he set out deliberately to do so. Mrs Siddons, as was the right of the great, commanded the Belfast company to her lodgings to run through a play before the evening performance. Most of the actors gabbled through their parts, as they do now at a word rehearsal. But Edmund, determined to be conspicuous, spoke his few lines with all the power at his command. When he had finished, Mrs Siddons complimented him: 'Very well, Sir, I have never heard that part done in that way before.'

In the summer of 1806, at Miss Tidswell's recommendation, Edmund was engaged at the Haymarket theatre in London. But only as a junior member of the company; he played such parts as a Servant, a Clown, a Goatherd, an Alguazil, Rosencrantz in *Hamlet* and Carney in *Ways and Means*. He used to complain afterwards that once at rehearsal, when he was trying to speak his lines as well and as tellingly as possible, the actors regarded him contemptuously and one of them sneered, 'Look at the little man, he's trying to make a part of Carney.'

In London, he realized now, a small-part actor was just a small-part actor, and it was a waste of his time to attempt to be anything else. If he looked ridiculous or spoke absurdly, then they would laugh at him, and if he forgot his lines or reeled on to the stage intoxicated, they would hiss him. But otherwise they would treat him as if he did not exist. They came to see the leading performer, and on him they would bestow all their praise or censure. It was the duty of small-part actors to play up to their star, to keep well out of his way and in no circumstances to intrude themselves.

Edmund found it particularly galling that at the Haymarket he had to kow-tow to Alexander Rae, who was entrusted with many of the leads in tragedy. Rae was a young man — only a few years older than Edmund — and he had had a comparatively quick rise to fame. A little while ago Mrs Siddons had played with him in Liverpool and she had thought him very promising. Now he was firmly established as a London actor, and though he would never be considered really great, he would remain until his death moderately successful and well-known.

Edmund had a special reason to resent Rae. He had known him in his childhood days. Rae's mother, who was matron of St. George's Hospital, was a friend of 'Aunt' Price, and the two boys had often met in 'Aunt' Price's back parlour. There as playmates they had acted scenes from Shakespeare and Edmund had far outshone his friend. Rae, in fact, had regarded Edmund almost as a maestro and had been content to listen to his instructions and abide by them.

But now that their positions were so completely reversed, Edmund was morbidly suspicious of Rae. One day at rehearsal he failed after several attempts to speak a line as Rae wanted it spoken. At last Rae remarked in desperation, 'Very well, Sir, we'll try it tonight,' and turned on his heel. A normal young man would have accepted this as a mild rebuke. But Edmund regarded it as an unpardonable insult which it was impossible for him to forgive or forget.

He would have liked to answer Rae back, but, however passionately he felt, he had no powers of repartee, fierce, cutting or flippant. He could only make a 'peculiar motion of his lips, as if he was chewing or swallowing' – and say nothing.

Only at the tavern could Edmund recapture a little of what to him, aged seventeen, was the glamour of his childhood. He did not go to Finche's, which was patronised by the smart London actors and was the social centre of the stage, where he would have been abashed in the presence of his superiors. He preferred the Harp or the Antelope. There circus men, unemployed strolling players, country managers and the riff-raff of the profession met together and drank far into the night. There players sought jobs from managers, and the managers drove hard bargains. At intervals some tipsy actor got up to recite or to sing a comic song or to give imitation of the famous. After a glass or two Edmund could conquer all his reserve and become as aggressive and overbearing as he yearned to be. Except by bombast, how was he to prove that he was really great and would one day, in spite of his present inferiority be acclaimed as such?

Edmund would far rather have starved as Hamlet than grown fat as Rosencrantz. During the next two years, he was the star performer in various small country theatres, and even returned to Sheerness for a while which he must have known was a retrograde step. In March, 1808, he joined the Gloucester Company and it was there that he met his wife.

Mary Chambers was considered an amateur, though she was given leading parts to play. She had no talent, and it is odd that she ever decided to go on the stage. She belonged to a respectable family in Waterford (Ireland) and must have been brought up to believe that the theatrical profession was next door to perdition. But, having arrived in England in the correct capacity of governess, she had grown weary of her humdrum existence. Paradoxically, she had risked the degraded status of strolling player in order to better herself. For she had realized that at twenty-nine if she were not married soon, she would never be married at all.

Mary was no beauty, but compared with Edmund she was extremely well-born. She was also an expert flatterer and a first-class audience. And he, after all, was her leading man. Every day he went to her lodgings and would recite and declaim for her especial benefit. With her he could be as vainglorious as he pleased. He would tell her of all his hopes and ambitions, and she appeared to believe in him as profoundly as he believed in himself. He soon supposed himself madly in love with her, not realizing that he was actually in love with his own reflection.

Though Mary had no critical faculty, she really did believe in him. He would, she thought, assuredly get on in his profession and be able to give her all the things she wanted — the things that came with wealth and position.

But she was the last woman on earth that Edmund should have married, if there were to be any chance at all of his avoiding disaster. Though she was a traitor to her class when she went on the stage, she still retained all her native instincts and prejudices. She was refined, priggish, proper and socially aspiring. She might, indeed, have made an excellent wife to a model husband. For she was sweet-natured and clinging and devoted, and she knew, in her unimaginative way, how to be a good mother. But she had no understanding of the waywardness of genius. She was not amusing or stimulating or managing or capable of any depths of feeling. In adversity she wasn't even loyal. She was just dull and woeful.

Did she really suppose that he would win success easily? That without any further effort from her he would remain as buoyant as he was now in the ardour of his young, imagined love? Presumably she must have done, though during the four months of their courtship she was given at least one warning of what kind of man it was she meant to marry.

It happened in Stroud whither the company had moved from Gloucester. Since business was proving appalling the manager decided to import a star attraction for two nights. He chose the infant prodigy, Master Betty, who was now seventeen and four years before had taken London by storm. Edmund was required to play Laertes to his Hamlet and Glenalvon to his Norval in *Douglas*. He did not refuse ostentatiously. He behaved as he did when he had felt insulted by the 'country gentleman'. He hid himself until he was sure that Master Betty had left Stroud. He had been sleeping rough, but he would not, so he told Mary when he turned up at her lodgings, suffer the degradation of being subordinate to that young impostor who had gone straight to the top without any real talent.

Mary listened without understanding, though she allowed him to believe that she was on his side. Perhaps she thought that as soon as he was married he would place his responsibilities as a husband before the satisfaction of his pride. If so, she was soon proved wrong.

In fact, his marriage merely intensified in him all those instincts which before had caused him so much anguish — his impatience, his arrogance and his passionate desire for recognition. Others, not much older than himself, and some even younger, like Master Betty, had already been acclaimed. Yet he after years on the road was still unknown. Though he had once liked to show off his versatility, he now thought it beneath his dignity to do anything but appear in the great roles of tragedy. And he had to put up with being ridiculed by some dunderhead critic such as the one who wrote of him in the *Staffordshire Advertiser*:

without energy, dignity or the advantages of a voice, he dragged through the heroic scenes with a dull monotony oppressive to himself and doubly so to the audience ... The performer's genius is nevertheless of an elevated cast — he is a good Harlequin!

He needed more than ever the encouragement that Mary, without realizing it, had been able to give him before she became his wife. But now that she was his wife, she could no longer pretend to sympathise with his extravagant restlessness and his insane vanity. She could not even listen to his troubles with a good grace. She expected him to think of his responsibilities as a husband instead of getting drunk 'to forget his sorrow', as she put it. Quite understandably, she abominated his drunken behaviour, but when she supposed that he drank to 'forget his sorrow' she showed how little she understood him. His sorrow (accepting the misnomer) was his power, the wild, ungovernable will to greatness without which he would never have triumphed. It tortured him only because it was frustrated. And he yearned not to obliterate it but to give it expression. Far from resorting to alcohol as a narcotic, he took it for what he believed it to be — a stimulant — and under its courageous influence supposed himself already what he longed to be.

Dissipation was not an end in itself. Even Mary realized that. She had not married just a weak, idle, bombastic, braggart, but a fierce genius who, in her own words, 'studied and slaved beyond any actor I ever knew'. 'He used to mope for hours on end, walking for miles alone, thinking intensely on his characters. No one could get a word from him.'

But he was studying for something more than to become a great actor. He was studying to take his place in the world as a great man. He didn't spend by any means all of his spare time in taverns; a good deal of it must have been spent in libraries. He wanted to improve himself. In his copy-books he set down simple phrases and translated them into Latin, Greek, Italian, Welsh and even Portuguese; he wrote down notes on history, natural history, geography and details of the lives of Isaac Newton, Cicero and Plutarch. All these scattered pieces of learning he tried to memorize, and often reproduced some of the Latin and Greek phrases in letters to managers and others. At the same time, these conscious efforts at self-education could take the form of pure fantasy. For example, Mary recalled that when he was with a company at Waterford, he used to carouse with some 'low friends' among the disaffected Irish (called Croppies) and she remembered how he swore that he was going to lead the Croppies to victory.

Mary outlived her husband by sixteen years, and during that time she had the field to herself. There is no doubt that she supplied Barry Cornwall, who wrote the first full-length biography of Edmund Kean, with a good deal of his material. I have seen one of her several letters to Cornwall, and almost everything in it is detrimental to Edmund's memory. Not surprisingly, therefore, the story of the Croppies is told in Cornwall's biography, but there is no suggestion that the copybooks existed. Nor that other of his accomplishments, such as his piano-playing, were worked at until near the very end.

Edmund, on the other hand, never said a word against his 'little Mary' and this despite the fact that his adored Aunt Tid strongly disapproved of the marriage and seemed determined from the beginning to break it up. In 1810, when he wrote to Mrs Clarke, he had been married nearly two years, and though he spoke enthusiastically of Mary's histrionic talents, she had in fact been demoted from her original position as leading lady because of her inability 'to support any line of business'. They were living in effect on his income of 25/– a week. And they were already three. For Mary had given birth to Howard Anthony Kean on 13th September, 1809. They had been through one financial crisis after another, accumulating debts wherever they went, and finally were compelled to walk all the way from Birmingham to Swansea so that Edmund could take up a star engagement in Andrew Cherry's company. Years later Mary could recall many of the nightmare incidents of that journey, which meant for her illness, hunger, continual anxiety and fear.

But Edmund was used to poverty, and he longed for money

only in so far as it was synonymous with power. The sufferings he endured during the long walk to Swansea from Birmingham were the least part of his troubles, and once arrived he was probably more at peace with himself than he was ever to be in the days of his great wealth and fame. His position in Cherry's company made him a local celebrity, and it brought him into contact with a number of people, socially and intellectually his superiors, who encouraged him to find other outlets, besides dissipation, for his frustrated energies.

Andrew Cherry himself, unlike the majority of country managers, was not a parsimonious, illiterate vulgarian who had built up a theatrical circuit for want of something better to do. He was an author with several published plays to his credit and he was an accomplished comedian who had, in his time, once graced the London boards. He was, besides, educated beyond the immediate needs of his calling, and consequently he commanded an unusual respect both from the patrons of his theatres and from the local Press. His circuit embraced Swansea, Camarthen and Haverfordwest in South Wales, and in Ireland Waterford and Clonmel. At each of these towns he could rely on an abnormal measure of support and approbation. For example, the Swansea newspaper *Cambrian*, in whose columns he was a discreet and consistent advertiser, praised him fulsomely; and towards the start of the present season wrote: 'Mr Cherry has on all similar occasions paid the strictest attention to the preparation of new pieces and placed them before the public in a style of theatrical correctness never before witnessed in the Principality, but on the present occasion we must declare his taste and liberality have gone hand in hand and he has produced *The Exile* in all that perfection of excellence which scenery, rich characteristic costumes, machinery and good acting can display.' That, at a time when it was customary to sneer at most country performances, was a glittering notice indeed. But little Cherry was a manager among managers. In Camarthen he was considered of sufficient eminence to be invited to the Mayor's annual dinner at the King's Arms; and there he raised half the sum of money necessary for building a new theatre.

Edmund, as leading actor of his company and also official 'getter up' of ballets and pantomimes, came in for a good deal of the Cherry prestige. Of his performance of Daran in *The Exile* the *Cambrian* wrote that 'he gave that mysterious character the full force of his assumed ferocity and the tender breathings of his genuine humility'; and of his first ballet, called *The Savages*, that 'it was prepared under the immediate direction of Mr Kean with an effect highly honourable to that gentleman's pantomimic abilities.'

Edmund must have felt that at last he had made an advance. He began expressing himself in doggerel — a habit he kept to the end of his days — and to develop his untutored talent for musical composition. He wrote a melodrama called *The Cottage Foundling*, or *The Robbers of Ancona*, which was performed on his benefit night. Afterwards he wrapped the manuscript in a large parcel and sent it to Aunt Tid. But, practical woman that she was, Miss Tidswell declined to pay the postal dues. So *The Cottage Foundling* disappeared.

The Company moved from Swansea to Camarthen to Haverfordwest and across the Irish Channel to Waterford, and then followed the same circuit again. It was in Waterford that Edmund wrote his melodrama, and it was there too that he met two people who were to be his life-long friends. The first was Thomas Colley Grattan, a man of many different professions, but then an eighteen-year-old subaltern in the town garrison. With that amused, indifferent, rather lackadaisical attitude which gentlemen affected towards country theatricals, he didn't arrive at the theatre until the Fifth Act of *Hamlet*, when the fencing scene was in progress. He noticed that Edmund — 'the thin, pale little man' — looked like a mere pigmy beside the handsome and very tall Laertes. But when Hamlet 'began to return the lunges *secundum artem*', Grattan was surprised to see 'the carriage of a practised swordsman'.

So he went round afterwards to see Edmund and tactfully suggested that Edmund should give him fencing lessons, which was strictly unnecessary as off stage Edmund was no more accomplished than he was himself. Nevertheless, he liked this little play-actor whose personality was somehow compelling and whose manners were agreeably modest and unassuming. And Edmund, for his part, was enormously gratified to find an 'officer and gentleman' who did not insult him but, on the contrary, treated him as an equal.

Edmund met another man in Waterford, who was to become his life-long friend, when Sheridan Knowles joined the company there. Knowles was far from the run of ordinary strolling players. He was the son of a lexicographer and himself had academic achievements to his credit. He had thrown up the chance of a prosperous medical practice to go into the theatre, and naturally he had done so in defiance of his family's wishes. But though he was stage-struck, he sought fame as a dramatist and not as an actor.

Knowles was essentially big-hearted and took an immediate liking to Edmund. They had things in common, these two poverty-stricken strollers. Both were ambitious, self-willed and determined and both were staunch believers in their own powers. But intellectually Knowles was far better developed than Edmund and morally much more stable. Ten years would pass before he won his first success in London with *Virginius*, and during most of that time he would earn an obscure if respectable living as a schoolmaster in Belfast and then in Glasgow. He would continue the while to write, of course. But he would await his opportunities patiently and well.

Knowles was another who bothered to understand Edmund; and his affection both for the actor and the man, despite one severe test, never wavered. At Waterford, he wrote a tragedy especially for Edmund which was performed by Cherry's company with eminent success. It was not a work of much note and didn't help to make its author's name. But Knowles never forgot it. In 1833, he acknowledged to the Edinburgh Shakespeare Club how much he owed to the encouragement of 'Poor Great Edmund Kean, that noble, enthusiastic, fine little fellow'.

Edmund spent two years in Cherry's company, and then during his second visit to Waterford something happened that Mary had been dreading all along. He had a serious quarrel with Cherry. What about is not known, but the probability is that he felt in some way affronted. Anyway, the Keans were left stranded in Waterford without money or even the prospect of another engagement. And now there were four of them. Their second child, Charles John Kean, had been born on 8th January, 1811.

They made just enough money out of a benefit performance in a Waterford assembly hall to pay for the passage across the Irish Channel, and reached Whitehaven in July of 1811. From there they set out for London. They had no means of support other than Edmund's ability to perform whenever or wherever he could find the opportunity.

They moved from town to town, always living on the verge of starvation, making a little money here and no money there, selling clothes in Whitehaven and books in Dumfries and their dog, Daran, in Penrith, often being scorned and persecuted and occasionally being grateful for chance generosity — vagabonds in truth. For five months they were subjected to this torture; they travelled on carts and wagons, stopping in squalid public-houses, eating bad food and too little of it, trying to quieten their two small children, who cried most of the time for want of proper care. Mary blamed Edmund entirely for their predicament. Although he was resourceful enough in the business of hiring a hall, arranging a programme, writing out playbills in his own hand, scouting around for local patronage, he was as blind as ever to his marital responsibilities. He still drank and swore and ran up debts. Her reproaches did nothing to reform him. They merely reminded him of his failure. In York he was driven so frantic by her recriminations that he tried to join the army. He was prepared to sell his destiny for the price of a common soldier's pay.

When they reached London at last in December, Mary could scarcely have been less likely to impress and conciliate the dreaded Miss Tidswell. She said much later that Aunt Tid peremptorily turned them out of the house and refused them help of any kind. In fact, she did not speak the entire truth. Aunt Tid certainly disliked Mary on sight so that Edmund had to arrange for his wife and children to stay with Aunt Price. But Aunt Tid had Edmund to stay, and though she refused to lend him money probably because she thought, in her uncompromising way, that this would be of assistance to his wife, she may well have been instrumental in getting him a job with Richard Hughes.

Richard Hughes managed the theatres at Weymouth and Exeter on behalf of his father — John Hughes — who was personally in control at Sadler's Wells, London. It was from Miss Tidswell's address in Tavistock Row that Edmund sent a letter to John Hughes from which the following is extracted:

> Having travelled lately some hundred miles with a large family and very expensive luggage, I am left in London in a situation (which many of our brother professionals are acquainted with) *Non est mihi argentum*! It is my wish, therefore, to depart by tomorrow's coach for Weymouth, but I frankly confess I at present have not the means; if, Sir, you would oblige me with the sum of ten pounds, Mr Finch or Miss Tidswell will become answerable for my immediate appearance at Weymouth, and Mr Hughes might proceed in the reduction of ten shillings per week till the debt is discharged. . . .

Miss Tidswell must have thought — she undoubtedly hoped — that Edmund would leave Mary behind in London to fend for herself. But, in fact, the Keans travelled to Weymouth together — presumably on a loan of ten pounds from Hughes, Senior.

They remained more than eighteen months under the son's management, moving from Weymouth to Exeter and from Exeter to Guernsey. They were richer than they had ever been before with Edmund being paid two guineas a week as the star performer, and Mary occasionally being called on to play small parts. But there was no happiness in this for either of them. Edmund was completely out of patience with the stroller's life, and Mary was perpetually nagging him to forget his pride and go back to London even if this meant playing secondary parts. In London, she thought, she would at least be able to make a home for herself and her children and live in some permanency — even security. Finally, Edmund gave in. He wrote to Samuel Arnold, the manager at Drury Lane:

> If the service of so humble a candidate for public favour would be accepted . . . I should be most happy in becoming a member of the new community . . . to be settled in the metropolis in a third or fourth rate situation sufficient to support my family with respectability would be the summit of my ambition . . .

He did not, of course, mean that. His ambition was still limitless, but when his letter was ignored he became even more certain that fate was permanently set against him. 'If I succeed,' he said, 'I shall go mad.' He could yell and bluster in taverns, but there was no one to whom he could turn for consolation or encouragement. He was alone in his failure and would be so in his triumph, which was now painful to contemplate for he could not persuade his conscious self that it would ever happen. He had been frustrated too long. In the provinces so few people understood great acting. And in London, where perhaps he might have been noticed even as Laertes or Richmond, he was not wanted.

Even his success in a world which was far too small for him was mostly of the kind that he resented. It was still the same. Audiences crowded to see his Harlequin, while they stayed away from his Hamlet. He said he never felt so degraded as when he had 'the motley jacket on his back'. On the stage he was 'all life and vigour — turning somersaults in the most graceful and astonishing manner, dancing to the delight of the house, and finally (his great feat) leaping through the face of a clock.' But beforehand in the Green Room, he had sat 'sad and depressed, awaiting his call, declaring he was stiff, and that it was impossible he could go through his part.' Afterwards, 'with a great coat flung over his patchwork dress,' he would seek balm for his lacerated feelings in the tavern. There among his fellow players and fellow tipplers he could rise, at least in his own estimation, far above the status of a provincial Harlequin. Harlequin! He'd be damned if he ever played the part again!

But he had to, for that was his value to Hughes. There was little response to his playing of tragic parts. When Lord Cork, a reputed connoisseur of the Drama, came to the Weymouth Theatre, he took no notice at all of Edmund's efforts to impress. 'Whilst I was playing the finest parts of *Othello* in my best style,' he said, 'my Lord Cork's children were playing at hot cockles in front of the box and Lord and Lady Cork were laughing at them.'

Mary, for her part, had lost all confidence in Edmund's future. Their sufferings, she said, had made him not wiser, but more impossible. Wantonly he threw away his chances and prejudiced his popularity. Nightly carousals, public brawls, scenes with outraged landladies — these were not enough for him. Quite often he appeared drunk on the stage, and sometimes did not appear at all. Then he had to apologise to his audiences and not very gracefully, for he had neither the art nor the nature to be contrite in public. And poorly attended benefit performances were the consequence.

When they reached Guernsey, he said, 'Mary, what do you think, I can get brandy here for eight-pence a bottle. I can drink it instead of beer.'

And in Guernsey he was finally sacked by the remarkably patient Hughes. He was cast for a part which he was determined not to play — Charles I in *The Royal Oak*, a piece which had been especially selected by some local celebrities. Characteristically, he got drunk on the night of the performance and sent a message to Hughes saying that 'King Charles had been beheaded on his way to the theatre.' Later, he turned up in the auditorium and started mocking Hughes, who was reading King Charles's part, with shouts of 'Bravo' until he was thrown out at the demand of an infuriated audience. Hughes with amazing generosity would have been content to fine Edmund two weeks' salary. But Edmund preferred to chuck up the job rather than swallow the insult of being punished.

So the Keans were back where they had been eighteen months before, except that this time Edmund went to London alone in search of a job. He left Mary behind in Guernsey with the children. Howard, at the age of three, was Mary's only means of livelihood. He was already beautiful and talented enough 'to gain a dinner for his parent'. He had appeared in ballets, and was called the 'pupil of Nature'. Edmund was fiercely proud of Howard. Maybe that was partially the reason why he had made up his mind to sacrifice all his hopes of becoming the theatre's greatest tragedian, or rather of being acknowledged as such. If he could earn the chance for Howard to be great — not on the stage, but in a far grander (and safer) profession — he would continue to clown, dance and sing for the rest of his life, and he would not feel debased.

He was in search of a job at one of the minor theatres. Only at the Patent Houses — Drury Lane and Covent Garden — was it possible for tragedies to be performed, except during the summer months when the Haymarket had a franchise. All other theatres were called minor and were debarred from performing tragedy or any play without music. Once again Edmund enlisted the help of Miss Tidswell, and she promised to use her influence with Robert William Elliston whom she knew as a member of the Drury Lane Company. For Elliston, besides being an actor, was a man of numerous other activities, and was, above all, a master showman. He planned in a few months' time to re-open the Olympic theatre in Wych Street.

In Guernsey, Mary wrote on 13th September to her friend, Margaret Roberts in Waterford, saying that she was ready to desert her husband. Would dear Margaret send her a trifle or at least advise her what to do? She was so miserable. Her tears blinded her. Should she return to Ireland and run a school? She was so wretched, she could not think clearly herself.

My first step to misery [she wrote] was going on the stage. I then married my husband — possessed of every talent requisite for his profession, educated to give grace to that talent, and could he have endured patiently a little longer, fortune might have rewarded his very great abilities. To forget sorrow he first took to drinking. Every dissipation followed of course. His nights were spent with a set of wretches — a disgrace to human nature. One step led to another, till inevitable ruin was the end.

But she didn't desert him, though she was still convinced that nothing but misery lay ahead of her. She and the two children joined him in Barnstaple, where he had taken a temporary job with Henry Lee's company, while he waited to find out whether his offer to join Elliston's minor theatre had been accepted or whether he was to suffer the ultimate humiliation of having even this sacrifice of his ambition rejected.

On 2nd October, 1813, he heard from Aunt Tid that Elliston was prepared to engage him to 'superintend the stage business' and to play all the principal parts for a salary of three guineas a week. At the time, he had no idea that an important man was working to promote his interests. He only knew that if he refused Elliston's offer, he would be failing his wife and children. So on the same day he wrote to Elliston:

> The terms I own do not bring my expectations to a level with the respectability of the establishment, but I place so firm a confidence in your reputed abilities that on the proof of my humble abilities and asiduity [sic] towards the general promotion of the business you will be inclined to increase it, that I accept your present proposals, simply requesting you to name the extent of the services expected from me and what time you expect me in London.

Thus he concluded a legally binding agreement with the manager of the Wych Street theatre, and at the time he had, dejectedly, every reason to suppose that he would fulfil it.

3

Dr Joseph Drury, the retired headmaster of Harrow, had been to see Edmund act in Exeter, and was one of the very few who found him an impressive tragedian. Indeed, he had introduced himself afterwards, and he took an almost paternalistic interest in the queer, untutored little man, who, it seemed to him, worked so hard, who was determined to get on and who acted with such fire and brilliance.

Dr Drury was an ardent playgoer, and a man of some influence in the theatre world. He knew the facts about the London Patent House — facts which were widely whispered, and printed in the Press for those who cared to read them. Covent Garden, under the experienced direction of Thomas Harris, with a first-rate team of actors headed by John Philip Kemble, was prospering. But Drury Lane was tottering towards bankruptcy. Its management under a Committee of Lords and Gentlemen was muddle-headed and disorganized. The Chairman of the Sub-Committee, Samuel Whitbread, though eminently successful in the brewery trade and laudably energetic in the House of Commons, knew nothing about the stage.

What Drury Lane needed above all else to restore it to favour was a new star of tragedy, and when Dr Drury found himself at a dinner party sitting next to Pascoe Grenfell, a member of the Sub-Committee, he started to tell him all about a wonderful young actor he had seen recently, named Edmund Kean. His words did not fall on deaf ears. Pascoe Grenfell began to make inquiries and to influence his colleagues and his chairman.

Edmund did not receive Drury's letter informing him of all this until after he had accepted Elliston's offer. Of course, he would allow nothing to stand in his way should anything come of Pascoe Grenfell's negotiations. But would they? So often he had hoped, fervently hoped, and as often been disappointed. Why should his accursed luck ever change? He boasted to Lee, who was his friend and supporter as well as manager, that he was going to Drury Lane. But he couldn't really believe it.

In fact, his spirits were at their lowest ebb. Howard was very ill, and needed every attention and luxury his parents could afford. They hadn't had enough money to afford to pay for the whole family to travel from Barnstaple to Dorchester by coach, so Mary had taken Howard with her, while Edmund followed on foot, carrying Charles on his back.

Mary had been reluctant to entrust Charles to his father's care, and she was waiting nervously when they arrived looking dusty, dirty and travel-stained. How could Edmund have neglected Charles so shamefully, she wanted to know? His clothes were absolutely ruined and they would never have the money to buy him new ones. Edmund answered wearily that she ought to be very thankful that they had arrived at all. It was typical of Mary to complain and go for him when he was worn out with fatigue.

Yet they were closer now than they had been for a long while — or would ever be again. At last they had an interest in common — anxiety over Howard. Mary nursed the little boy and Edmund stayed with her gazing silently at the child who was suffering so much. He could scarcely tear himself away to go to the theatre. It was such pain to sing and dance and make them laugh while he was loaded with the secret fear that his adored son was dying.

On 15th November, he was acting Octavian in *The Mountaineers*. The house was nearly empty, but he noticed a stranger sitting in a private box, who seemed anxious and attentive and unlike an ordinary provincial. Afterwards, while he was changing for the ballet of *The Savages* in his dressing room below the stage, he overheard a conversation about himself between Lee and the stranger. 'Kean,' Lee was saying, 'a wonderfully clever actor. He is going to London.' 'Certainly, he is clever,' replied the stranger, 'but he is very small.' 'His mind is large,' Lee countered. When Edmund reappeared, the stranger congratulated him on his performance. Edmund said, to keep up appearances, that he would not be in Dorchester for long, since he had signed a contract with Samuel Whitbread. But the stranger was uninterested in Edmund's pathetic bravado. He wanted to talk business. 'My name,' he said, 'is Arnold. I am the manager of Drury Lane Theatre.'

Edmund, to use his own words, staggered as if he had been shot. He did not know where he was or what he was doing. He could hardly get through his part in *The Savages*. But it did not really matter. The business was as good as settled. He was to be given a trial in one of the famous roles of tragedy on the stage of Drury Lane Theatre. Only the financial details — of small concern to him — remained to be discussed over breakfast at

Arnold's hotel next morning.

Now at last he could come home to Mary with news which would wipe out all the bitterness and the recriminations of the past. She had not believed him, but he had always known he would succeed. He had justified himself, and she would admit it just as the world would admit it too. 'My fortune is made,' he told her, 'my fortune is made.'

He had forgotten Howard, or rather, perhaps, had assumed unconsciously, that the same change of fortune that had brought Arnold to Dorchester had also cured his son. But now that he saw the sick child lying there, in pain, just as he had left him only a few hours before, he wondered whether he would ever know complete peace. Yet surely Fate could not be so cruel as to give with one hand and take away with the other. Howard would live — he must — to share in his father's triumph.

Edmund did not go to bed that night. But neither did he join his drinking companions. He stayed awake, thinking of his performance of Octavian, brooding over setbacks in the past, imagining achievements in the future and talking joyously to Mary, as he had done in the days of their courtship, talking in fact to himself.

Next morning he kept his appointment with Arnold.

On 20th November, Arnold reported to the Drury Lane Committee that he had concluded an agreement with Mr Kean, 'an actor of great promise', from the beginning of next month 'upon terms which he considered very advantageous to the theatre — to wit, £8 per week for the first, £9 per week for the second year and £10 per week for the third.'

On 21st November Edmund wrote to Dr Drury telling him the story of the last few days and expressing, in a gloriously belaboured mélange of English and Latin, his joy and his ever-lasting gratitude.

And on 22nd November, Howard died.

Possibly, Mary suffered as much as Edmund. But even if the death of her elder child was her supreme sorrow, she painted it in colours no more and no less vivid than all the rest of her woes. She was a woman who liked to wallow in her misery, and she herself said she could never be happy except in 'writing or thinking of that Gem who was 'cold, cold in the earth'.

> It changed his golden locks [she wrote to her sister, Susan] changed very much a few hours before he died ... as I left Dorchester where he is interred, as I gave a last look at his grave, my heart strings cracked, my soul, my happiness lay entombed there. As it was the last experience I was at with him, I had him carried to his last home as well as I could. His coffin was handsome, an angel bearing an infant, the plate on it — his name and age. I got up to see him carried out. Four girls dressed in white bore his coffin, others all white, strewing flowers; while he, the loveliest flower, was insensible to all. No mourners had he — no tear wet his grave. I could not see the earth laid on the sweetest child ever mother had ... As we took leave of his corpse, his angelic countenance, with that look of his glory and seraphic smile it ever possessed seemed to say, 'Mama, I grieve for you — but do not grieve for me — you know not how happy I am.'

Edmund's outward display of grief was terrible while it lasted. On the night of 22nd November, Mary feared he was going off his head. He looked on his dead child and burst into a flood of wild, uncontrollable tears. He rushed out of the house to drink, and discovered there was not enough brandy in the world to dull his pain. He returned home to rage and swear that it was impossible Howard had gone, and that he would bring him back to life. But next morning he awoke (according to Mary) more composed. And two days later on 25th November he wrote to Dr Drury a very simple, touching letter, free of Latin phrases. It read:

> The joy I felt three days since at my flattering prospect of future prosperity is now obliterated by the unexpected loss of my child.
> Howard, Sir, died on Monday morning last. You may conceive my feelings and pardon the brevity of my letter.
> This heartrending event must delay me longer in Dor-

chester than I intended. Immediately I reach London I will again, and I hope with more fortitude address you. In the midst of my affliction I remember your kindness and with greatest respect sign myself, Yours, etc, E. Kean.

It is certain, at least, that whichever of the two of them suffered the more, they could not share their grief. The funeral took place on 24th November. On 29th November, Edmund gave his last performance in Dorchester. Next day he left for London, determined that Howard's name should never be mentioned in his presence again. He took with him the good wishes of his fellow-actors, particularly of Lee who had made much on the Dorchester playbills of Mr Kean's forthcoming debut at Drury Lane. He was twenty-six, though in spirit more than twice that age. He was embittered, heartbroken by the death of his favourite son and physically weakened both by want and by dissipation. But after eight years of strolling he had at last schooled his passion to serve his trade. He had longed to be great; and he had learned how to be a great player.

4

Though Edmund's triumph was now assured, nearly two months of agonising frustration and near-starvation lay ahead of him.

He had not completely forgotten about his contract with the Olympic. He had written to Elliston on 19th November:

Sir, since I last wrote to you, I have received a very liberal offer from the proprietors of Drury Lane. It gives me unspeakable regret that the proposal did not reach me before I had commenced negotiation with you; but I hope, sir, you will take a high and liberal view of the question when I beg to decline the engagement for Little Drury. Another time I shall be happy to treat with you.

Now Elliston probably didn't care two pins whether the little actor from Dorchester came to the Olympic or not. Nor would it have been of much benefit to him to have a tragedian at the Olympic — even one who was being talked of as a 'phenomenon'. But Elliston had a contrary nature and was also a man of considerable *amour propre*. The dramatic change in Edmund's fortunes gave him an opportunity too good to be missed. He replied at once calling Edmund a deserter and loftily reminding him of the contract which he (Elliston) intended to enforce.

Edmund thought that Drury Lane would protect him, but he was soon disillusioned.

'Young man,' Arnold said, after Edmund had been refused his second week's salary, 'you have acted a strange part in engaging with me, when you were already bound to Mr Elliston.'

This was a cruel and unexpected blow. He had thought everything was settled when Arnold welcomed him 'with more than common appearance of pleasure' and he was handed his first week's salary of eight pounds. He had only to await patiently the night of his appearance as Shylock, the part he had chosen for his debut. He was living in 'expensive' rooms at No 21 Cecil Street which he had taken, on the strength of his expectations, for himself and his family.

All he could do was to appeal once again to Elliston. 'The fate of my family is in your hands,' he wrote. 'Are you determined to crush the object that never injured you?' He went on to misquote Virgil and to conclude rhetorically:

... Am I to be cast again into the provinces, the rejected of this great city, which should afford a home to industry of every kind? With my family at my back I will return, for the walls of Wych Street I will never enter.

To this Elliston replied:

Sir, to any man with the smallest gift of intellect and the dimmest sense of honour it must appear that on 11th November, and previous to that time, you deemed yourself engaged to me, and that subsequently a more attractive offer having been made, you held it convenient to consider a pledge as idle as words muttered in a dream. To your rodomontade I send nothing in reply, and your Latin Hexameter I beg to present you with again as it may be useful on some future occasion.

All my engagements are made and fulfilled with honour on my part, and I expect an equal punctuality from others!

Later, a tripartite meeting was arranged among Edmund, Arnold and Elliston. It resulted in an apparent deadlock. Elliston talked so volubly that nobody else could get a word in. Arnold, formal and frigid, explained that though Mr Kean was undoubtedly under contract to the Wych Street theatre, he was also a member of the Drury Lane company and would, therefore be injuncted from appearing anywhere else.

Edmund was stranded in London without money or friends. Even Aunt Tid avoided 21 Cecil Street like the plague, for she would not meet Mary under any circumstances. But for the generosity of his landlady, Miss Williams, who 'somehow believed that he would be a great man', it is likely that he and his family would have died of starvation. It was the coldest winter on record — the winter when the Thames froze over.

The dispute dragged on for more than three weeks. And then, as if for no reason at all, Elliston suddenly made that grand gesture which he had intended to make from the outset. He agreed to forgo his claim to Edmund's services. He was doing well enough at the Olympic, in fact remarkably well, with a couple of performing dogs.

But Edmund's troubles were still not over. He wrote to Dr Drury at the beginning of January:

Mr Arnold told me he could not mention my name at the Treasurers . . . without a written document from Mr Elliston which that gentleman promised he would give me . . . Friday 24th from ten till three I was employed in running east, north, west and south of this city after Mr Elliston. At three I fortunately encountered him . . . and received from his own hand the required document and hastened overcome by fatigue and anxiety to Mr Arnold. I could not see him then, therefore sent in my name and *lex scripta*. For nearly one hour I waited in the passage with the rest of the menials of the theatre and had the mortification of seeing them all conducted to his presence before myself, and when summon'd at last to appear, was with the continued brow of severity informed that I had no claim on the Treasury, my engagement had all to begin again.

Actually, Arnold must have valued Edmund's services, and the Committee, too, were counting on him to make a hit, for paragraphs had appeared in the *Morning Chronicle* to that effect. But in view of the way he had been treated, he could not understand why he had been brought to London in the first place. He believed that everyone at Drury Lane was intent on humiliating him. They laughed at him, mocked him, made fun of his small stature and his sad eyes, his lack of star quality and his dejection, his miserably shabby appearance. They called him 'the little man in the capes' because of an unwieldy garment he wore to keep out the cold.

He would never forget these insults. But equally they only increased his determination to succeed. His ambition was now a mania. He did not need the urgent advice of Dr Drury, 'bear all, bear all, only come out', for in the midst of his anguish, mental and physical, he could say, 'Let me but once set my foot before the floats and I'll let them see what I am.' His triumph would be his revenge on all those who had dubbed him 'Arnold's hard bargain' and had foredoomed him to failure.

The day arrived at last — 26th January, 1814 — when the Drury Lane playbills carried a notice of *The Merchant of Venice* with Mr Kean in the part of Shylock — 'his first appearance'. Though the Thames was beginning to thaw the sun did not shine that day, and very few ventured to Drury Lane in the evening. The house was, in fact, less than a third full. Dr Drury, with a party of friends, was there to applaud his protégé. William Hazlitt had come to represent the *Morning Chronicle* and had instructions from his editor to be as kind as possible to the new actor. He and the emissary of the *Morning Post* were the only professional critics present. Miss Williams was in the pit. Her lodger had been sent a whole pile of free passes or orders, as they were called. He had burnt fifty of them.

On the stage an actor looked through a peephole in the curtain, and saw that the audience was very small.

'What can you expect?' he said. 'There will be nothing till half price.'*

Edmund, overhearing this, interpreted it as a deliberate affront — another indication of the hostility of his fellow actors and of the world's indifference to him. But now he had finally become master of his own destiny, and he knew he could not fail. He had had one rehearsal — that same morning at twelve — to familiarise the Drury Lane actors with the bare routine of his performance, for that performance was exclusively his own work and would be judged as such. During the greater part of the nineteenth century, the producer (or director as he has been called in imitation of the Americans since the second world war) was a completely unknown figure in the theatre, so that there was no one to suggest to Edmund how he should speak his lines or to direct his movements. However, J.R. Raymond, the stage manager whose duty it was to marshal the crowds and to ensure that the small-part actors played up properly to their star, objected to at least one piece of Edmund's stage business.

'It is an innovation,' he said. 'Depend upon it, it will not do.'

'I wish it to be so,' Edmund replied. 'If I am wrong the public will set me right.'

His whole conception was an innovation. But Raymond couldn't have guessed that. At the rehearsal he had deliberately mumbled through his part. He was still oppressed by a sense of grievance, and he believed that the more unexpected his triumph, the sweeter would be his revenge. He seemed depressed, and didn't behave like a star. He chose to share a dressing room with some of the supernumeraries.

'Last Music' was called and Edmund already stood in the wings, awaiting his first entrance. Naturally, they had little or no confidence in him behind the floats. The strange, morose

---

* After the main play of the bill was finished, the prices were customarily reduced.

Edmund Kean as Shylock, January 1814.

Kean after an oil painting by George Clint.

little man did not resemble a tragedian. He looked so pathetically insignificant. Besides, as Shylock he was quite wrongly
made up. Instead of being the dirty, repulsive stage Jew, who
always wore a red Judas wig, he appeared almost Christian-
like in an ordinary black wig — and with his face clean and his
costume tidy. Whether he'd dressed in this way out of ignorance
or deliberately to flout tradition really made no difference. In
either case, he was courting disaster.

But in front they saw him for the first time when he stepped
on to the stage, and then he was miraculously transformed. He
was no longer the insignificant little man, the miserably in-
congruous 'candidate for public honours'. He was the histrionic
mesmerist and the complete master of the scene. He came
forward and bowed gracefully, and they were impressed. He
took up his position, leaned on his cane, gazed at Antonio,
and Dr Drury, anxious, knew that his protégé was safe. The
black eyes, which were to be famous, had already begun to
work their magic. Before he spoke a word, Edmund Kean
captured his audience.

And when the performance was over, and Hazlitt was on
his way to tell the readers of the *Morning Chronicle* that 'no
actor had come out for many years at all equal to him', and the
small house had cheered itself hoarse, Dr Drury went behind
the scenes to congratulate Edmund, expecting to find him the
centre of adulation. But for Edmund, apparently, the evening
was over. He was hurriedly changing back into his day clothes,
and preparing to leave the theatre as unobtrusively as possible.
He was not in the mood for a celebration of any kind.

He had determined not to give any hint of excitement until
he got home. And though he must have been wildly elated, his
elation was not of a purely joyous or thankful kind. He was to
prove himself incapable, now that he had won his long-sought
triumph, of looking forward without looking back. He could
not forgive or forget. In a sense, he could not think of the
future except in terms of the past.

He was not like those who in their days of ease and luxury
and recognition are content to ignore whatever lies behind
them. Nothing would ever obliterate from his memory the

sufferings and insults to which he had been subjected along his road to fame. Nothing, equally, would make him heedless of the occasional kindnesses he had received.

He meant to repay them all. His success was a weapon in his hands for vengeance — or as such he meant to use it. He would give Mary the things she had always craved, the things she had always whined for: wealth and finery and position. He would have Charles educated as a gentleman. But he would do all this out of pride, not love. He would do it as vengeance for past hardships and past affronts.

He rushed into the living room at 21 Cecil Street, and at last spoke a little of his pent up excitement. 'Mary,' he said, 'you shall ride in your carriage and Charley shall go to Eton.'

He might have added, for therein lay the core of his human tragedy, 'And now I'm acknowledged as a great actor, I shall force the world to treat me as a great man.'

PART TWO
Fruits of Triumph

1

Edmund Kean's triumph, allowing for the comparative slowness of communication in Regency London, was very soon complete. A month after his debut Arnold told a meeting of the sub-Committee that 'Mr Kean had performed the characters of Shylock and Richard III and had succeeded beyond the capacity of any actor within his recollection.' This was no exaggeration. At the second performance of Richard crowds stormed the doors of the theatre, and the free list was suspended whenever he was billed to appear. The official box-office returns were approaching £600: a figure that had not been dreamed of since the opening of the new building three years before.

By the time the season was over, he had added four other characters to his repertoire: Hamlet, Othello, Iago, and Luke in *Riches*. He had saved Drury Lane from bankruptcy. More than that, he had fulfilled a national demand. The romantic movement was at its height, and a great personality was needed on the stage to do for the histrionic art what Byron and Shelley and Keats were doing for literature. Edmund could call himself the true representative of Shakespeare's heroes.

John Philip Kemble, of course, was still at Covent Garden, but Kemble belonged to another generation and was nearing the end of 'his long reign'. He personified a cold, formal, declamatory style of acting — the Classical School as it was called. In himself he was a habit, and playgoers would remain loyal to him — more or less — for the brief remainder of his career. But the tradition that he represented was clearly doomed by 'the electric flashes of Edmund Kean's genius', to quote Hazlitt, 'having swept through it, like lightning withering without actually destroying a stately grove.'

If Kemble was still the king of the British stage, Kean was the heir apparent and already was enjoying many of the privileges of sovereignty. The Drury Lane Sub-Committee increased his salary to £16 per week for the remainder of the season, £18 per week for the next season and £20 per week for the three seasons following. As he was free to take provincial engagements when he was not working at Drury Lane, and could name his own figure, he was soon earning the huge income of £10,000 a year.

All this is not meant to suggest that Edmund was universally acclaimed. The diehards, still devotedly attached to the classical tradition, denounced him as a cheap impostor, and though they were far outnumbered they managed to make their voices heard above the general chorus of praise. They became not merely his detractors but his 'enemies'. For the stage was regarded almost as a prizefight ring in which leading players of the day battled for supremacy — with the minimum amount of good feeling. Consequently, partisanship was apt to be fierce, even violent.

And yet it is surprising how little diehard antagonism to Kean was reflected in the newspapers. Essentially, of course, he was the favourite of what one might call the Left-wing Press. Hazlitt of the *Morning Chronicle* and the critic of Leigh Hunt's *Examiner* (Leigh Hunt himself was in prison for criminal libel) welcomed him with an almost political fervour, if only because of his challenge to the artificial school of acting. Both these passionate apostles of truth showed their hand from the beginning. Hazlitt revelled in the performances of an actor of whose death scene in *Richard III* he could write: 'He fought like one drunk with wounds, and the attitude in which he stands with his hands stretched out after his sword had been taken from him had a preternatural and terrific grandeur as if his will couldn't be disarmed and the very phantom of his despair had the power to kill.' And the critic of the *Examiner* was even more wholehearted in his enthusiasm than Hazlitt. He summed up the feelings in his previous eulogies of Kean when he wrote, '. . . his Iago is, we think, the most perfect piece of acting on the stage; it is the most complete absorption of the man in the character.'

The *Morning Post* did not lag far behind when it described his speaking of the soliloquies in *Hamlet* 'as the workings of nature itself'. Even the *Times*, steadfastly conservative as always, had to admit that in spite of his many faults and his marked inferiority to Kemble, he was 'evidently a player of no ordinary cast'.

That, perhaps, was the weakness of his opponents' position. He could not be ignored or dismissed in a sentence. He had, of course, to suffer the shafts of criticism, for no critic who valued his reputation for impartiality was content to record empty gush or meaningless generalization. They examined every one of Kean's performances in the minutest detail, for, as I have said, he was all they were interested in and everything he did on the stage was to his credit or discredit. For example, Hazlitt pointed out that in the tent scene of *Richard III* he stood for a while as if in a reverie, drawing lines on the ground with the point of his sword, before suddenly recovering himself 'with a good-night to his lords'. And in *Hamlet* he did not make the usual definite exit after bidding Ophelia 'To a nunnery, go', but returned impulsively to kiss her hand and then hurried off the stage. Hazlitt selected that 'as the finest commentary that was ever made on Shakespeare'.

Even so Hazlitt had some fault to find with his interpretation of Richard and even harsher things to say about his Hamlet, which was too 'strong and pointed'. Since each critic had his pet prejudice, it was inevitable that what appealed mightily to one, appalled another. What the *Examiner* praised as 'animation', the *Times* condemned as 'lack of dignity'. But however much opinion might differ about his particular merits he was at least the centre of the controversy. There was commonsense in the following letter which appeared in the *Examiner* on 1st March, 1814:

Sir,

I am afraid you may consider a newspaper an odd place for the advice which I wish to give you which is not to mind what the newspapers say. A morning paper says — 'The

frequent smile which Mr Kean wore in Richard destroyed
the dignity that belongs to the character.' Says the evening
editor — 'Mr Kean forgot to diversify the sullenness he wore
by the spirit of coarse merriment with which Richard con-
templates the success of his projects.' A weekly publication
states that Mr Kean's 'extreme decreptitude in Shylock cast
an air of imbecility over the malice of the character;' but
a lively wag in a magazine writes — 'Mr Kean should not
make old Shylock trip across the stage with a step light
enough for Gratiano' . . . If you will just allow me to remark
your tone and manner in the third scene of the fourth act
of . . . but why should I make remarks which I have just
advised you not to attend to . . .?

2

What sort of actor, then, was Edmund Kean? The answer to
that must largely depend on intuition, and on which part of
the evidence of the many people who actually saw him and
have written about him one prefers to believe. But one thing
is certain. Those who say — and there are many of them —
that if Kean could be resurrected, he would be laughed off the
stage, are talking nonsense. The circumstances and conditions
of theatrical production are, of course, very different from
what they were in Kean's day. But any actor worth his salt
can adapt himself to change just as Charles Mayne Young and
Macready had to adapt themselves to the revolution for which
Kean himself was responsible.

Moreover, if one is going to believe Kean would be useless
in these theatrically enlightened times, one must also consider
that Hazlitt was a fool to admire him. Yet very few of us
would care to argue that there is a dramatic critic alive today
who approaches Hazlitt's stature.

In my belief — and I'm supported in this by a memory of
Macready's — Edmund, though a talented child, was not a
great actor born but became one as a result of his overwhelm-

ing urge towards greatness.

Macready as a schoolboy saw Edmund act at Birmingham when he was still an unknown strolling player. Later, Macready recalled the experience in these words: 'A little mean-looking man in a shabby green satin dress (I remember him well) appeared as the hero, Alonzo the brave. It was so ridiculous that the only impression I carried away was that the hero and heroine were the worst in the piece'. How little did I know (or could guess) that under the shabby green dress was hidden one of the most extraordinary theatrical geniuses that have ever illustrated the dramatic poetry of England.'

That impression was not exaggerated or inexpert. Macready was the son of a provincial manager, and was to become one of the great actors of the nineteenth century. The truth is that Edmund Kean worked and slaved, as well as drank and mixed with admiring prostitutes, because in spite of his birth and early environment, he was not extraordinarily gifted. All his innovations of style were the superb devices by which he overcame his initial handicaps — of voice and person and figure.

He certainly did wisely to choose Shylock for his debut. It was a part that hid his physical disadvantages, and yet it gave him boundless scope to exploit those brilliant artifices by which he overcame them. It was unnecessary, in any case, to be an Adonis to act the Jew. But he showed his audience a Shylock such as they had never seen before — not just a stage 'prop' but a man who felt and hated passionately, who inspired pity as well as loathing and fear as well as contempt. He brought all his art into play in order to produce these effects — his energy, force and agility; his impassioned yet strictly disciplined use of speech and gesture and movement. He acted not only with his voice but with his whole body, especially with his eyes, which fierce or tragic, frightful or melting, could express as much in a moment as most actors could describe in a night.

His purpose was to create an immediate sensation, and Shylock suited that purpose to perfection. The part is not long nor does it require much sustaining, but it provides opportunity to rise suddenly, amazingly to greater and greater heights. And that was Edmund's *forte*. Coleridge said that he revealed Shake-

speare 'by flashes of lightning'. The very way in which the
story of Shylock is developed boldly, swiftly, dramatically,
enabled Edmund's lightning to flash with increasing frequency
and each time with more brilliance.

By the same token one feels that his choice of Richard III
as the second character in which to show himself was extremely
fortunate, though he himself was not as confident of success
as he had been when he appeared as Shylock. He was suffering
from a bad cold, and he was fearful that he might fail as Richard
and thus be dismissed as just a flash in the pan. He insisted on
a public apology being made for him, and Richard Wroughton,
one of the Drury Lane actors, came forward to explain that
Mr Kean was 'very much indisposed'.

But there was no real need for anxiety or fuss. Edmund
spoke with a hoarser voice than usual, but he brought Richard
III to life. It was one of his finest parts, and one can understand why, for it offered him opportunities to display the
whole range of his virtuosity — his violent passions, his panther-
like gaiety — opportunities in other words for his lightning to
flash.

With Shylock he had unlocked the gates to recognition;
with Richard he banged them wide open. And his success in
every character he chose to play for the time being now seemed
assured. Hazlitt hailed him as a naturalist — a throw-back to
the glorious days of David Garrick. Hazlitt meant that he was
in revolt against the Classical school, as personified by John
Philip Kemble, whom Hazlitt called 'an icicle on the bust of
tragedy.'

Was Edmund really a naturalist? Not, presumably, in the
modern sense. He said himself once, with becoming candour,
that he never 'felt' a part unless he was acting with a pretty
woman, and he revolted against the Classical school only because he knew that he lacked the qualities to succeed in it.
Moreover, he played to rule just as surely as Kemble did, even
though the rules were of his own making. He was extraordinarily
methodical. He never made a move or gesture that had not
been carefully thought out. George Vandenhoff, another
well-known actor, who in his youth had first-hand memories

of Edmund, wrote of his Othello that his inflections and intonations never varied. They 'might almost have been read from a musical score. And what beautiful, what thrilling music it was! The music of a broken heart — the cry of a despairing soul!'

Nevertheless, in parts that suited him he does seem to have given the impression, as presumably Garrick did, not of acting a part but of being it. And this must mean that he had developed during the years of his preparation for greatness a superb technique that enabled him to disguise not so much *what* he was doing but *how* he was doing it: how, for example, he contrived to appear tall when he was, in fact, too small for most parts. He could not be considered in any way a forerunner of Stanislavski and the Method. Nor, of course, could Garrick. Incidentally, Garrick's widow, who was approaching her ninetieth birthday, became one of Edmund's greatest admirers, though she did not hesitate to tell him in what points he was inferior to her David.

Most of those who saw him, including the critics, eventually reached the conclusion that he was not good at sustaining a long part; that he was apt to be careless, hurried, inaudible sometimes in the quiet, explanatory passages. Restraint was alien to him. Essentially, he was 'flashy', 'all energy and passion', and he needed the big scene to show off his real powers. And then, apart from his small size, which did not really fit him to play the great parts, he was handicapped by a voice which was not naturally melodious. Though he could command it as he pleased, it was often hoarse and grating: Leigh Hunt, after he came out of prison, decided it was 'somewhat between an apoplexy and a cold'.

And yet, at the beginning, he was the master on the stage; his personality was dazzling and secure. The brilliant throng who flooded the vast Drury Lane auditorium whenever he appeared, sat in suffocating airlessness, with the stink of burning candle-wax in their nostrils (a little later it would be gas fumes), but Edmund could still them into silence or melt them into tears or rouse them to frenzies of applause almost at his will.

Crabb Robinson, who kept a diary, saw Edmund for the

first time as Richard and though he admitted that 'he played the part better than any man I ever saw,' he harped a good deal on his defects. 'His most flagrant is want of dignity, he projects his lower lip ungracefully ... his declamation is very unpleasant. He gratified my eye more than my ear. His speech is not fluent, and his words and syllables are too distinctly separated.' But a few weeks later Crabb Robinson was swept off his feet by Edmund's Othello. 'It is the character for which he is least qualified, but one in which he has most delighted me ... I could hardly keep from crying ... It was pure feeling.'

That is what impressed his admirers most — his ability to make them forget he was really an undersized little man with an unmelodious voice. Perhaps he was particularly suited to be Richard or Shylock or Iago; perhaps there needed to be something warped or deformed or monstrous in a character to hide his physical defects completely and to give his powers full scope; perhaps his best performance of all was as Richard, which allowed him to show off 'that tempest and whirlwind of the soul, that life and spirit and dazzling rapidity of motion, which filled the stage, and burned in every part of it.' Yet as Hamlet, in spite of his essential lack of nobility, he revealed beauties before undreamed of. As Othello, especially in the scenes of pagan and heartrending pathos, he seemed, as it were, to rise up out of himself and to become, in truth, the noble Moor of Venice. And as Macbeth, his acting after the murder of Duncan was judged by Hazlitt to be one of the two finest things he had so far seen him do; 'The hesitation, the bewildered look, the coming to himself when he sees his hands bloody, the manner in which his voice clung to his throat and choked his utterance, his agony and tears, the force of nature overcome by passion — beggared description. It was a scene which no one who saw it can ever efface from his memory.'

At any rate, as I have already said, I suspect that Edmund Kean was the greatest actor who ever lived. It cannot be more than a suspicion, and my justification for it comes largely from some words written by Thomas Colley Grattan. He said that while Byron was a fantastic imitation of Napoleon, Kean was an absurd one. Kean could have done nothing else but go on the stage. Suppose the same thing had been true of Napoleon, suppose all Napoleon's immense ego had been confined within the tiny orbit of the theatre, suppose instead of making the world his stage he had been obliged to make the stage his world, might he not have given performances of unimaginable greatness? I think he might, and I believe Edmund Kean did. The most striking evidence of this came when in 1816 he played the part of Sir Giles Overreach in *A New Way to Pay Old Debts*. The audience might have laughed at this little man pretending to be the archvillain who at the end of the play, when he is cornered by his enemies, threatens them with these words:

> . . . Shall I then fall?
> Ingloriously and yield? NO: spite of Fate
> I will be forced to hell myself,
> Though you were legions of accursed spirits
> Thus would I fly among you.

His audience did not laugh. They were, for a moment, speechless with real terror. Lord Byron was convulsed and several ladies in the boxes fainted. Even the actors — hard-boiled professionals, jealous of their own rights — showed clearly enough that they too were frightened. And then the pit rose in a body and cheered and went on cheering. Next morning Hazlitt, for once robbed of any critical faculty, wrote:

> There is something in a good play well acted, a peculiar charm that makes us forget ourselves and all the world. We cannot conceive of anyone doing Mr Kean's part of Sir Giles Overreach so well as himself. We have seen others in the part, superior in the look and costume, in hardened, clownish, rustic insensibility, but in soul and spirit, no equal to him. He was not at a single fault. The conclusion was quite overwhelming.

Surely no one can seriously believe that a man like Hazlitt was

so unsophisticated and barren of taste that he would have
confessed himself overwhelmed by acting which a modern
audience would consider merely 'ham'.

3

Mary, of course, was completely transformed.

Marriage with a starving genius had been no fun at all, but
she adored being the wife of a man of immense means and
position. At least for a while she supposed that she did.

Her triumph was really as great as his. She had stuck to him
through all the years of misery and illness and poverty, in
spite of the one occasion when she had nearly run back to
Ireland; and now at last she had what she wanted. She wasn't
selfish with Edmund's money. She sent immediately for her
sister, Susan, to come and live with them. The whole Chambers
family were to have a share in the spoil. Old Mrs Chambers,
living in Waterford, was given a new house, a new wardrobe
and anything else she fancied. At No 21 Cecil Street bank
notes were piled high on the mantelpiece and Charles played
with golden guineas on the floor, 'Riches, unlooked for riches,
pour in on them daily,' wrote Susan. 'She will be as rich as a
Jew!'

Mary, dressed up to kill, had plenty of opportunity to try
out her social gifts. Every day, morning and afternoon, distinguished callers alighted from their carriages at No 21 Cecil
Street. There were those who wished to pay their respects to
the great actor; there were those who simply had a curiosity
to see what he looked like off the stage; and there were the
individual members of the Drury Lane Sub-Committee, Samuel
Whitbread, Pascoe Grenfell, Douglas Kinnaird and Lord Essex,
who came, under the guise of flattery, to give him their advice.

Mary was the hostess who received her husband's grand
friends, and she seemed to them a sweet little suburban house-
wife, not brilliantly intelligent, but touchingly proud to be the
adoring wife of a celebrity. Thomas Colley Grattan, who

called to renew his acquaintance with the Keans a year or so later, was particularly impressed by Mary's 'warm-hearted and overflowing recognizance of ever so trivial a kindness, or tribute of admiration offered to "Edmund" before he became a great man.'

Mary looked forward to a lifetime of buying and spending, of rubbing shoulders with Lord This and Lady That, of dining out here and there, of entertaining the 'best people' at her own table, of being, in fact, the wife of a great tragedian. And at first she had no reason to suppose that Edmund would spoil it for her. Success had none of the effects that it usually has on men of his kind. Arnold at the end of the opening season was able to report that 'he had conducted himself with the greatest propriety'. And outside the theatre, in spite of all the fuss that was made of him, he remained modest and unassuming. 'He is a simple man,' said Douglas Kinnaird, 'he sent his wife to Pascoe Grenfell, his patron, to ask him if he thought it would be any presumption or impropriety in his keeping a horse. Grenfell said no, and his partner Williams sent him one that cost eighty guineas.'

But already by January 1815, a year after his Drury Lane triumph, it became clear that things were not what they seemed. It was then that a certain J.H. Merivale, a fervent amateur of the drama and a playwright in his spare time, wrote to Dr Drury, asking him how he could contribute to the 'good work' of rescuing 'poor Kean' from 'the imminent dangers which beset him'. Merivale had been to see Mrs Kean who received him 'with a hearty shake of the hand', but with a great deal of embarrassment. Edmund, she told him, had gone hopelessly astray. About a fortnight ago, he had written to her from Woolwich saying that he'd made up his mind never to see her or Charles again; that she could take all the money and that he would find freedom in some foreign country. She instantly went to Woolwich with her sister and found him 'surrounded by all his most pernicious associates'. She couldn't deal with him at all, but a day or two later he returned, and was extremely contrite.

That sort of incident — and there were others of the same

kind — made Mary very unhappy, and she poured forth her
tales of woe to Lady Elizabeth Whitbread and Lord Essex and
anyone else who would come to her assistance.

She put a good deal of the blame on Miss Tidswell, who she
believed was deliberately exerting an evil influence on Edmund
to injure her. But though Mary was desperately anxious to safe-
guard the actor's success, she had no more understanding of
the man than she had ever had. She was possessed of all the
snobbish instincts of an exalted suburban. She worshipped the
trappings of gentility. Within eight months of confiding in
Merivale, she had decided that Cecil Street was not a grand
enough environment for her, and she persuaded Edmund to
rent a large, handsome house in Clarges Street, Mayfair, the
very hub of the *beau monde*. In October 1815, they took up
their abode.

Mary could now receive her guests, not in a slum, as it were,
but in her own rarefied setting. With Susan to help her, she
settled down to live the life of a famous man's wife. After
Edmund's huge success as Sir Giles Overreach, Susan wrote
excitedly to Margaret Roberts . . . 'We got a present of a hare
and two pheasants from Lady Elizabeth Whitbread yesterday
and today Mr Maxwell sent us a Hare and Brace of partridge,
which we keep for tuesday (sic) when Mr and Mrs Grenfell,
Mr and Mrs Utterson, Mr and Mrs Bush and Miss Brown, Mrs
Blackman, Mr Dinman, Mrs Plumptre & a Miss Maxwell dine
here. . . .'

Everything was done very properly — trained liveried servants, high-class cooking, refined conversation and polite
formal dinner parties attended by as many nice and celebrated
people as possible. She expected Edmund to sit at the head of
his table and to entertain his distinguished guests as best he
could. Though there were violent quarrels and times 'when he
went off his head', he still had too much family loyalty to
break away completely. He was always contrite in the end, and
so Mary pursued her way relentlessly, without regard to him,
only pausing to wonder plaintively why he was so impossible
and why he was so set on ruining her happiness.

For his part, he found the Clarges Street house alien to him, and he came to regard Mary and Susan Chambers not as allies but as enemies. They were two against one. They would be three against one, when Charles grew up, for Charles, unlike Howard, was his mother's son, and she was turning him into a proper little prig. There was no place for Edmund's tavern cronies at Clarges Street. He was invited to dinner parties and the like by the nobility, but he was sensitive enough to realize that 'they meant him no honour by these distinctions, which were so many negative tributes to their own importance.' Their manner towards him was condescending and class conscious. He complained that they did not treat him as an equal, but as a kind of wild beast on parade. They hardly addressed a word to him except on the subject of acting, and even then they seemed more concerned to express their own opinions, which he considered unmitigated nonsense, than listen to his. Invariably, he was left unnoticed after they had done with praising or criticising his latest performance, for they went on to discuss politics and painting and endless other topics of which he knew nothing. He listened to their interminable talk in moody silence, and began to feel that though he had worked hard all his life he had learned nothing, and that though he had travelled all his life he had been nowhere.

Naturally, he turned away from such people who made him so acutely conscious of his own shortcomings. It was not a privilege to consort with them. It was an intolerable humiliation. But he was a king among the whores, bruisers and assorted riff-raff of the tavern, and he was loyal to them. Mary had her way in most things, but she could not persuade him to desert them. On the contrary he clung to them more fiercely than before. In time, he came to look upon himself as an outlaw from society and was consumed with a longing to get his own back on a world which had no use for him or his companions. He would be vociferously anti-social. He would show those who scorned him that even though he could not shine as a conversationalist he was none the less a man of no ordinary cast. In short, he would force them to take notice of him.

In his efforts to build up his personality, he became what we should now describe as a ravenous publicity-seeker. He was no longer at pains to conceal his Napoleonic complex. On the contrary, it is because he was so determined to attract attention to himself, that so much is known about his eccentricities.

He kept a pet lion, which, so it was reported, he controlled with his eye, just as he hypnotised audiences when he was on the stage. He was an ardent amateur of prize-fighting, and knew how to use his fists in an emergency. He owned several wherries, and instituted an annual boatman's race. He retained the service of a private secretary — a certain R. Phillips — who looked after his arrangements at Drury Lane, communicated on his behalf with the Press, accompanied him on his provincial tours and — probably his most important duty — attended him at the tavern. But for a stage player to employ a private secretary, whatever the real nature of his duties, was quite unheard of.

He was the founder and President of various fancifully named 'communities', the most famous of which was called the Wolves Club. The Wolves were sworn to detest class distinctions and to 'damn all lords and gentlemen'. Organized gatherings gave a purpose to Edmund's carousals and made the tavern more surely his kingdom. Although they seemingly provided him with the excuse to end many bacchanalian nights under the table, he regarded them with monarchical gravity. His opening speech to the Wolves Club ended with this plea: 'It is my hope that every Wolf oppressed with wordly grievance, unmerited contumely or unjust persecution, with heart glowing with defiance, may exclaim, "I'll to my brother, there I shall find ears attentive to my tales of woe, hands open to relieve and closed for my defence." '

Understandably, no doubt, the Wolves Club acquired a nasty reputation in the outside world. It was alleged that Edmund had founded it for his personal protection and that its members were sworn to boo every rival tragedian off the stage. That probably was quite untrue. But what 'unmerited contumely' or 'unjust persecution' had he to fear?

In his insensate desire to appear important — a great man — Edmund allowed himself to be identified with his extravagancies, so that he became known as ludicrously vain and over-

Edmund Kean as Richard III.

Cruikshank cartoon of Edmund Kean as Richard III.

bearing. Yet, in his heart, he knew his own weaknesses, and tried to curb them. He was by no means the unspeakable vulgarian that he chose to paint himself. Drink was a habit of very long standing. During his strolling-player days he had wasted many hours in the tavern, but he had also worked hard and he had had to do so in order to reach his present eminence. His genius was not a gift from the gods, nor were his 'flashes' the inspirations of the moment. He was able to show Douglas Kinnaird five hundred pages of comments he had made on Shakespeare.

Even now between his orgies and his ravings against a social order, he set out to employ his leisure wisely. He practised his piano playing, cultivated his love of music, enlarged his knowledge of classics and learned how to phrase a letter. He had the same appetite for education, for rising above the status of a pothouse actor, the same inquisitive mind, the same longing to be the equal, or indeed the superior, of any man of culture as always.

But though he possessed qualities in plenty, he failed abysmally to make proper use of them. His most ferocious detractors did not deny that he could be both brave and generous. But his courage was too often misplaced and his generosity was far too impulsive and disorganized to earn him much credit. After he became the 'first actor' at Drury Lane all manner of unworthy acquaintances, whom he had met in taverns and elsewhere, came to fawn on him, to cash in on his success, to drink and be fitted out at his expense. He was not the man to ignore them. He was not the man even to ignore Nance Carey, who turned up soon enough with a grown-up son and daughter-in-law and a grown-up daughter. It is doubtful that he welcomed her with open arms, but at least he gave her an allowance, and made some efforts to help her in her desultory career. Then there was Aunt Tid. Edmund felt bound to reward her. It was just unfortunate that she had better opportunities than ever now to make trouble between him and his wife.

'By God he is a Soul,' said Byron, and Byron, unlike the majority of his class, tried patiently to discover the soul of the actor in the man. He would invite him to small dinner

parties and would encourage him to talk about his strolling
player days. At the end of the evening, after the bottle had
been passed round freely, he would persuade him to give his
imitations of Kemble, of Incledon, of Master Betty and the
rest. But none of this was what Edmund really wanted. The
time came when, according to Thomas Moore, 'Byron was
offended at Kean's leaving a dinner which had been chiefly
made for him . . . Kean pretended illness and went away early;
but Byron found out afterwards that he had gone to take the
chair at a pugilistic supper.'*

When Mary spoke of his 'contrition', she undoubtedly spoke
what was true. But Mary also told Samuel Whitbread on one
occasion that her Edmund was 'the best man in the world'.
She didn't honestly believe that. She didn't have any idea what
sort of *man* he was or how he should be handled. Possibly, the
only person in the world who understood him was Aunt Tid.
But her one concern was to separate him from Mary, and
though she helped to do this, the final result was disaster.

4

Already in his first season at Drury Lane, Edmund was cough-
ing up blood. He spent the summer fulfilling provincial engagements, and on his return Hazlitt publicly reprimanded him.
'We see no reason,' he wrote, 'why he should make himself
hoarse with performing Hamlet at twelve o'clock and Richard
at six, at Kidderminster . . . To a man of genius, leisure is the
first of benefits as well as luxuries.'

But in Edmund's view there was an excellent reason. He
wanted to make hay while the sun shone. He was haunted by
the fear of slipping back to what he had been, and that is why
he could never allow himself to be outshone in a direct con-
frontation with a rival.

---

*   *Memoirs, Journal and Correspondence of Thomas Moore*, edited by
      Lord John Russell. 1853–6.

Already his star had been partially eclipsed by the emergence of a young lady at Covent Garden, named Eliza O'Neill, whose Juliet had been acclaimed a masterpiece. Edmund was forced by the Drury Lane Committee to offer comparison with her by playing Romeo, a part to which he could hardly have been less well qualified to attempt. He could neither look like a boy nor could he simulate the ardour of young love. In years he was certainly youthful, but in spirit he was very mature. He did not understand how to woo and he had no sympathy with Romeo's calf-like devotion. He acted as if he were forcing himself to speak lines with a show of conviction which really made him blush so that his performance far from revealing nature, was essentially anti-nature. According to the critic of the *Sun* '. . . He exaggerated every passion and tore them to tatters.' And Hazlitt, though he found two particular pieces of Kean's acting quite admirable, was very critical of the performance in general. Romeo was Edmund's first failure, and he must have been thankful that he did not have to play the part opposite Eliza O'Neill's Juliet.

One may see from his performance of Macbeth the kind of tricks he used to keep all the focus on himself. His Macbeth was strong and powerful — so much so that he dominated the play; and that does not often happen even when Lady Macbeth is given to an actress of inferior quality. Edmund stole her thunder; the following extract from an anonymous letter which appeared in the *Champion* shows how he did it:

> . . . Let me remark a most important difference between the acting of Mr Kemble and Mr Kean. To Lady Macbeth's question 'when does Duncan go hence?' [sic] Mr Kemble replies indifferently 'Tomorrow as he purposes'. With Mr Kean it assumes a very different aspect. In an emphatic tone, and with a hesitating look . . . he half divulges the secret of his breast . . . 'Tomorrow as he . . . *purposes* . . .'

In other words, by means of a pause and a stress, he gave the impression that the idea of murdering Duncan had already occurred to him. From then on he appeared not the pawn of his wife's ambition but the master of his own destiny. His performance did not appeal to any of the critics as his best. Hazlitt described it as sketchy. At the same time, he considered his acting after Duncan's murder one of the two finest things he had yet done:

> The hesitation, the bewildered look, the coming to himself when he sees his hands bloody, the manner in which his voice clung to his throat and choked his utterance, his agony and tears, the force of nature overcoming passion — beggared description. It was a scene which no one who saw it can ever efface from his memory.

Still, it was inevitable that someone would eventually come along to challenge Kean on his own ground. In October 1816 he was somehow prevented from fulfilling an engagement to appear as Sir Giles Overreach at the Brighton theatre; and consequently an unknown actor from Worthing named Junius Brutus Booth was called in to take his place.* The audience expected to be bitterly disappointed, but ended by deciding that Booth was every bit as good as Kean himself.

The news reached London. On 12th February, 1817 Junius Brutus Booth made his debut in *Richard III* at Covent Garden. His success was instantaneous, and no critic failed to comment on the resemblance between him and Kean, though there was dispute as to whether he was an original or a mere imitator. Only a meeting between the two of them could decide the issue.

It happened very shortly. Booth had a dispute with Covent Garden over money, and Drury Lane was delighted to snap him up so as to arrange the histrionic battle of the century. Whatever Edmund's views were or might have been on the subject, it took place on 20th September, 1817. Booth was Iago; Edmund Kean played Othello.

That night the Drury Lane stage became a kind of prizefight ring; and the auditorium was filled to overflowing with

---

*   Father of the famous Edwin Booth and of Abraham Lincoln's assassin, John Wilkes Booth.

excited, wildly cheering spectators. Booth was the challenger with everything to gain. Kean was the champion whose title was in jeopardy. Booth was the sentimental favourite. The odds were about even.

Or so the spectators had decided. But the contest eventually proved a very one-sided affair. 'On entering, Mr Booth was welcomed by thunders of applause,' wrote the *Morning Post*.

> He commenced his performance with great success. But as the play advanced he lost the high ground on which he had stood; and the comparison which the audience were increasingly called upon to make was not very favourable to him. His Iago was ... nothing like a too sanguine public had fondly anticipated ... In some of the most interesting scenes his labours were witnessed with the most perfect serenity, and a most appalling calm prevailed where heretofore we have been accustomed to look for a storm of approbation ... With another actor in Othello, the Iago of the evening might have been thought great, but by the side of Kean we could discover nothing original in thought, vivid in conception or brilliant in execution ...

Booth had fought his hardest. But Edmund had been by far too good for him, had made him look puny. He had risen to the occasion in a manner that was terrific, frightening and quite unforgettable. He had suspected — probably quite rightly, for he was already beginning to acquire an unsavoury reputation outside the theatre — that there were many in the audience who would enjoy seeing him vanquished. So he had come upon the stage determined to prove to the public, once and for all, that he was the one and only Edmund Kean, and that there was not another actor in the world to touch him.

He fought with a great show of sportmanship. At the end of each scene, he bowed and smiled and took Booth by the hand and affected to believe that the huge applause was meant for both of them. But while the play was on, he fought in deadly earnest. He gave no quarter. He never allowed his opponent an opening:

... Up and down, to and fro he went, pacing about like a caged lion, who had received his fatal hurt, but whose strength was still undiminished. The fury and whirlwind of his passions seemed to have endowed him with supernatural strength. His eye was glittering and bloodshot, his veins were swollen and his whole figure restless and violent. It seemed dangerous to cross his path and death to assault him. He was excited in a most extraordinary degree as though he had been maddened by wine.

Edmund's Othello must have been a gigantically selfish performance. But its effect was overwhelming. It swept all the other players — including Iago — clean off the stage. And once again, as had happened when he first played Overreach, even the actors were moved. As one newspaper reported: 'A comedian, a veteran of forty years' experience, said afterwards: "When Kean rushed off the stage in the third act, I felt my face deluged with tears — a thing that hasn't happened to me since I was a crack, this high!" '

A few of the critics next morning tried to make out that Booth had lost only on points. But the majority stated what was true — that he had been well and mercilessly slaughtered. At any rate he did not come back for more. Though *Othello* was announced for repetition on Saturday, 26th February, he pleaded indisposition, and afterwards crawled back to Covent Garden, claiming that he had been fouled. It was even suggested in one newspaper that the members of the Wolves Club had pledged themselves to drive him from the stage.

There is no doubt that Edmund lived in terror of being overshadowed by another actor and his behaviour on the stage was, to say the least, megalomaniacal. Booth was to appear again with him several times in the future. But not as a serious rival. In one memorable night Edmund Kean burst the Booth bubble.

In the years that followed, he was obliged to fight off other challengers for his crown, but none whom he defeated so devastatingly as the first of them. If he was a selfishly unscrupulous type of actor, and almost certainly he was, he must be forgiven for his determination to hold on to a position that he had struggled to attain for so long and so hard. He was, as he frankly said, terrified of losing it. And he must be forgiven on the same grounds for other similar offences.

From the time of Samuel Whitbread's death in July 1815, the fortunes of Drury Lane had been declining rapidly. Edmund, who had at first created a very good impression with his employers by his apparent willingness to accede to their wishes, latterly became extremely rebellious and did pretty well as he liked. The new plays selected by the Sub-Committee were of a very poor order, with Kean playing in them only if he approved of the leading part, and things came to a head when a tragedy in five acts, called *Switzerland*, was unveiled on 15th February, 1819. The author, Miss Jane Porter, was a distinguished novelist, but she had no experience of writing for the theatre, and had contrived to write an excessively cumbersome and boring play. The audience responded as audiences were apt to respond throughout the early part of the nineteenth century if they did not like what they'd been offered. During the last two acts they shouted so loudly and yelled 'Off, off' with such vehemence that the actors could not make themselves heard. At the end of the play pandemonium broke out. And no semblance of peace was restored until the manager appeared to announce the withdrawal of *Switzerland*.

Unfortunately for Edmund, however, Miss Porter, who had a literary reputation to keep up, refused to lie down under so crushing a humiliation. She maintained that her play had been ruined because Edmund had given such an atrocious performance and furthermore accused him of having done so deliberately because he had been forced against his will to appear in the part by the Sub-Committee.

Miss Porter's assertions — she even maintained that she had insisted on withdrawing the play — were little more than the hysterical whinings of a disappointed author. Nevertheless, when the weekly papers appeared, it was clear that she had won powerful support. The critic of the *Champion* under the heading of 'Conduct of Mr Kean to Authors, Proprietors and the Public' claimed 'undeniable authority' for stating that

Edmund had not bothered to learn his lines, that he had embarrassed the other actors by perpetual inaccuracies and 'with arrogant carelessness, he had talked through his character, like a washerwoman over her tub.'

> But if [the critic continued] [Kean] bashaws it — alike to actors, managers and authors, and will suffer no other merit, among the first, to appear beside him on the boards — no production of the last to be accepted or to succeed, that does not make his character the exclusive object of *attraction* and no wish or promise of the second to be fulfilled that does not chime in with his ambition to shine, not only superior but alone, it is high time for criticism to look to the other side of the picture ... William Hazlitt wrote him up: let him take care that he does not put himself down.

In a sense the *Champion* had a good case. Edmund's personal popularity, or rather his 'pull', was no longer strong enough to keep Drury Lane above water. During the past three years he had had only two genuine successes and (apart from his tried characters) had appeared in flop after flop. *King John*, which he had produced on 1st June, 1818, had been so disastrous a failure that the theatre had to be closed for three nights afterwards.

But if it was true, as he boasted both in public and in private, that he had little regard for the authority of his employers (the Sub-Committee), that he was his own master and that his 'reason was his will', it is inconceivable that he could have been forced to play in a tragedy he disliked and equally inconceivable, for a man who was intent on safeguarding his reputation as Britain's 'first actor', that he should deliberately have acted it badly. Though the house was often half empty on the nights that he appeared, on other nights it was emptier still. His value to the box office had lessened certainly; but that was not because of his refusal to cooperate with second-rate dramatists but rather because of his inability to judge the merit of a play as opposed to that of a part, which is a common fault of many actors, especially star actors.

Before he had had time to recover from Miss Porter's fulminations, he was made a target for abuse by another outraged author. Charles Bucke had written a tragedy called *The Italians*. It had been accepted by the Drury Lane Sub-Committee as long ago as the autumn of 1817, but — much to Bucke's disgust — had never been produced. Bucke now seized the opportunity to publish it together with a long preface in which he accused Edmund of perfidy. He alleged that Edmund, after giving him a 'positive assurance that nothing should prevent' the play from being performed, had deliberately used his influence to have it shelved indefinitely, because he had been dissatisfied with the part intended for him and had feared that the other characters 'would excite too much interest'.

Bucke's statement was probably true in essence, but if Edmund had simply ignored it, it would have attracted very little attention. Charles Bucke was an author of no distinction and *The Italians* happened to be a very poor play. But instead of maintaining a dignified aloofness, he rushed headlong into print with an extraordinarily offensive letter that was published, simultaneously, in all the leading newspapers:

On reading *The Tragedy of Deranged Intellect* [for that was the name the play was known by in the Green Room], to my professional brethren, the only feelings it excited were uncontrollable laughter, and pity for the author. From this criterion, I took the liberty of suggesting to the management the impossibility of producing a play, which must have been attended with considerable expense, when there was not in it one gleam of hope for its success. There is certainly some pretty poetry in the character which was to have been sustained by Miss Cubitt; and after that I will say in good set terms Mr Bucke's tragedy is the worst of the bad. In this opinion I am joined by the whole of the dramatic *corps* who were to have been concerned in it ... The publication of *Deranged Intellect* is all the answer necessary to the author's attack on my judgement; and for his inventive fabrication I publicly tell him that he has not uttered one word of truth in the whole of his aspersions, and I thus leave him to his

contemplation, with disgust for his falsehood and pity for
his folly.

If Edmund had wished to injure himself, he could hardly have
done so more effectively than by that coarse and common
letter — the response of a born gutter-snipe. It turned a minor
fracas into a sensational quarrel. It gave boundlessly more
scope for his enemies to attack him. It aroused widespread
sympathy for Bucke, who was rather a pathetic person, poverty-
stricken, with a wife and children to support. And it alienated
those who normally would have come to Edmund's support.
Even the critic of the *Examiner*, while defending him in prin-
ciple, felt bound to remark, 'The spirit evinced by Mr Kean
throughout the business has not been in good taste.'

It was no wonder that the public was enraged. No wonder
that Sir Walter Scott wrote furiously: 'how much do you
think I could relish being the object of such a letter as Kean
wrote t'other day to a poor author, who, though a pedantic
blockhead, has at least the right to be treated as a gentleman
by a copper laced, twopenny tearmouth, rendered mad by
conceit and success?'

And no wonder, when Edmund next appeared on the Drury
Lane stage he was greeted by hisses and loud cries of 'Off, off.'
He didn't attempt to speak the opening lines of his part, but
moved instead towards the floats, and addressed the audience:

'I apprehend that the interruption given to the performance
is owing to an opinion entertained by some that I have failed
in my duties to the public to whom I owe my reputation and
existence ... If in consequence of an unjust accusation I have
been betrayed for a moment into passion or ill temper it is the
fault of my nature — I cannot help it; but having done so, it
remains for me to apologize to that Public whose support I
now claim.'

That speech was not nearly humble enough to satisfy the
gentlemen of the Press, who thought Edmund owed a grovelling apology to Bucke. But it satisfied the audience who allowed
him to resume his part. He was seemingly forgiven.

When *The Italians* was finally produced with another actor

in the leading part that had been intended for Edmund, it was a
total failure, and provided Edmund with all the answer that
had ever been needed to Bucke's complaint. As it was, Edmund
had damaged his reputation with the Press still further, and
had added incalculably to the number of those who would
kick him without mercy when he fell.

Meanwhile Drury Lane was now £80,000 in debt and both
creditors and shareholders alike had reached the limit of their
endurance. On 4th June, 1819 the Sub-Committee resigned
in a body. On 12th June, it was announced that the theatre
was to be let to an independent manager. On 7th August, the
following notice was published in the Press:

> Mr Elliston has the honour to inform the public that he
> has become the lessee of the Theatre Royal, Drury Lane, for
> fourteen years. All letters respecting engagements should be
> directed (post paid) to Mr James Winston at the theatre.

Edmund had wanted Drury Lane for himself. He had promised
to devote all his energies to restoring its fortunes, and he had
offered to pay a rent of £10,000 per annum. He had looked
forward eagerly to being at last the ruling King of his own
Kingdom. Now he had been turned down in favour of Robert
William Elliston, the cause of all his wretchedness when he
first came to London. He determined never to enter Drury
Lane again so long as Elliston was in command.

Besides, there was a very attractive alternative. He had been
offered a small fortune to tour America, and he'd virtually
made up his mind to accept the offer. He was weary of the
attacks on him by the Press, and weary, too, of being taken
for granted by the public in London. He longed for the extravagant admiration which, he was sure, would be his again if he
could appear before vast new audiences who had never known
such acting as he would be able to show them. On 21st July,
he had written from York to his friend, Michael Kelly, the
famous singer and composer:

> Jack's* married — can you do anything for his wife, he says

---

*   Probably Jack Hughes, his friend from his strolling player days.

you can send her to Bath. I know you will if you can. He
lives at 35 Southampton Street. I am taking in the natives
of York in the very first style of swindling.

Shall quit England for America by the end of September.
When I go I shall delight myself in the recollection of many
pleasant hours I have enjoyed in your society, and wishing
you health, happiness and all the blessings in the world, I
sign myself,

Your very Sincere Friend
Edmund Kean.

Of course the chance of acquiring Drury Lane for himself, of
having a kingdom over which he could not only reign but rule
unchallenged, had been too good for him to ignore; but now
that his offer had been rejected, he decided that he would
go to America as he had planned. He was blissfully unaware
that the man who had frustrated him once would be perfectly
capable of doing so again.

5

Robert William Elliston had achieved the ambition of a lifetime.
He was at last the Great Lessee. He had renounced all his
other enterprises (including the Olympic), with the exception
of his provincial theatres, in order to become the manager of
Drury Lane. And now, with the instincts and energies of a
super-showman, he lost no time in making a tremendous splash.
Money was no object. He redecorated the theatre. He bought
tons of new scenery. He engaged an exceptionally strong
company of tragedians, comedians, singers and dancers — at
exceptionally high salaries — and was himself ready to continue
as a Drury Lane actor. He lined up a number of well-known
dramatists to whom he paid handsome advances on account of
future royalties. And he took good care to announce that
everything had been carried out 'under his personal direction'.

On 30th September he gave a reception to two hundred

distinguished guests. They stood up while the Drury Lane vocalists, led by the famous singer Braham, sang the National Anthem in unison. Afterwards they adjourned to the theatre saloon, where they were all entertained by the Great Lessee to a Ball and Supper.

Elliston never ran short of projects, and even on this night of triumph he had a few regrets. It was a pity, for example, that he had been unable to tempt Mrs Siddons from her retirement. It was a pity he had failed to persuade Sir Walter Scott to write a tragedy for him. It was, furthermore, most regrettable that he had not been able, for lack of time, to reconstruct the interior of the theatre at a cost of £7,000.

But, on the whole, he had every reason to feel proud of himself. Though building operations had had to be postponed until next year, the architect, Mr Beasley, had completed his plans, and a model of his design would be on show in the saloon throughout the coming season. The Great Lessee hoped that, among those who would see it, there might be a few professional men who would acquaint him with their expert opinions.

Elliston could count it among his major achievements that he had retained the services of Drury Lane's first actor, Edmund Kean, despite the latter's determination to go to America. For Edmund had overlooked one vital consideration — his contract, which still had a year to run. If he broke it, he would be liable to pay crippling damages. The only alternative would be to persuade the Drury Lane management to release him voluntarily from his obligations. But unfortunately for him he was now faced, not with the feeble opposition of a vacillating committee, but with the purposeful resistance of Robert William Elliston.

Against this formidable opponent Edmund had been powerless when he was unknown, and was soon to discover that he was still powerless in the days of his great fame. At first, he tried with a show of ill-natured bravado, to present Elliston with a *fait accompli*. He wrote in a long letter that his plans were already made and that he could not possibly alter them. Perhaps, after his return from America, he would enter into fresh negotiations to act at Drury Lane, but for the moment he had decided irrevocably to 'allow the field open to his compeers'. (Had not Elliston engaged Vandenhoff,* 'an actor of the first consequence', who would be able to play all the leads in tragedy?) 'Richards and Hamlets', he concluded in his most catty style, 'grow on every hedge. Grant you may have a good crop of them.'

Elliston, not in the least perturbed by these blundering tactics, was content to remind Edmund of his contract. Edmund offered to pay £1,000 forfeiture. Elliston promptly refused it. Edmund then toyed with the idea of breaking his contract regardless of the consequences, but when his legal advisers pointed out to him that the consequences would be, at the minimum, £10,000 worth of damages, he realized himself that 'it would be madness to embark for America'. On 27th September Mary informed Elliston that although her husband was at present in Scotland, he would return to his engagement at Drury Lane immediately after the first week in November.

Elliston, scrupulously courteous from the outset, was magnanimous in victory. He announced Edmund's name on the playbills in extra big lettering, and ignored the protests of several newspaper critics, who objected to this new-fangled *starring* system. He gave him *carte blanche* to spend as much money as he wanted on scenery, costumes and effects. He consulted him about casting. He even engineered a little indirect flattery, for when Horace Twiss was about to publish his *The Carib Chief*, Elliston demanded that the following paragraph should be included in the preface: 'The author cannot allow this play to be hurried through the Press without recording his tribute of admiration to the splendid exertions of Mr Kean, by which its unprecedented success has been achieved.' Considering *The Carib Chief* had been produced under the Sub-Committee's management and had been a dismal failure, that was typical of Elliston's method of handling Edmund.

It almost certainly did not win the approval of James Winston, Elliston's house manager, upon whom the responsibility of running the theatre seems to have largely devolved. His diaries,

*   John Vandenhoff, father of George (see p. 56).

partially written in code, tell the unhappy story of Drury Lane while Elliston was its lessee from 1819 to 1826, and continue for the year following. The diaries certainly deal very harshly with Edmund Kean, but it should be noted that they deal even more harshly with Elliston. He is pictured as being absent from the theatre most of the time, of being a drunken fornicator when he was there, of being wildly extravagant and in short quite mad. For instance the entry for 21st July, 1824, reads:

> Notwithstanding Mr Elliston's high talk last night of compensation etc., etc., from Kean ... he ... was this day humbugged into an engagement of £1,000 to Kean for eight weeks' performance of twenty-three nights. After this can anyone think him sane?

Yet later all was forgiven, and Winston was made the executor of Elliston's will. Whether Winston ever had kinder thoughts about Kean is unknown. The first entry that concerns him is for 8th November, 1819,* and reads:

> *King Richard III*: this tragedy was produced with entirely new scenery, dresses, and decorations. Every means was resorted to to ascertain at the British Museum, the Tower, and Herald's College, the proper costumes. The play was thus expensively produced for the purpose of introducing Mr Kean to the town under new management. Kean, being disappointed in obtaining the theatre, soon after announced his intention of not fulfilling his article transferred with the lease and going to America which, after mature consideration, he declined and returned to his Drury Lane engagement.

The first scandalous entry, partially in code,* is dated 17th January, 1820. It consists of a number of unsubstantiated allegations, which have already been quoted. But to repeat them, it says, first, that Edmund requested that the rehearsal of next evening's play should be delayed until twelve as he intended to get drunk that night; secondly, that he himself had said that he frequently found three women to 'stroke'

---

* See appendix.

during performances and that two waited while the other
was served; thirdly, that Samson Penley, an actor employed
at the theatre, had formerly seen Anne Storace, a vocalist
with the company, waiting for her turn. And finally that
'this night' (i.e. 17th January) he had Miss Smith, a small-part
actress, though he was much 'infected'.

The second scandalous allegation followed next day (18th
January). It says:

> Kean came about ten half-drunk. Elliston and [?Kean] in his
> dressing room got very drunk and about twelve o'clock got
> Mrs Middleton* in Russell's† room where they [Kean and
> Mrs Middleton] were locked up for half of an hour. He
> [Kean] borrowed of Elliston £5.

And the third, dated 5th June, 1820 reads: 'On Kean being
asked by Russell whether he would require to wait long between
Acts [of *Richard III*] he said, "No, not now, his *bubo* was
broken" — same evening a woman was waiting.'

It was this last sentence that Raymund FitzSimons, who
made the diaries the centre piece of his biography of Kean,
alleges Winston recorded 'with disgust'. FitzSimons also alleges
that 'prostitutes thronged his [Kean's] dressing room'. But that,
though very possibly true, would appear to be merely a deduction. I can find no evidence of it in the diaries.

Now before considering the question of whether such accounts
of Kean's misbehaviour were correctly stated, I must go back a
few years to September 1816, when Edmund had what was,
undoubtedly, the most fateful and fatal meeting of his life. He
was appearing at the theatre in Taunton, and on the night he
acted Othello a lady sitting in one of the private boxes was
apparently so overcome by his performance that she fainted.
At his suggestion she was carried across the stage to his dressing
room, where she rested until she was sufficiently revived to be
taken home. Next day her husband called on Edmund at his
lodgings. He introduced himself as Robert Cox, thanked Edmund
profusely for his kindness and consideration and suggested that

---

*   Drury Lane actress.
†   Samuel Russell, Drury Lane stage manager.

they should renew their aquaintanceship in London.

Robert Albion Cox was a native of Dorchester, where he had once been a banker and where he still owned a family estate. He was now middle-aged, and as a Londoner he was a man of some standing, though of no great fortune. He was a City Alderman and one among the numerous celebrities who served on the Drury Lane general committee. In May of 1818 he would be appointed auditor of the theatre. And in June of the same year he would be elected to the Sub-Committee in place of Lord Yarmouth.

His wife, whose maiden name was Charlotte Newman, was twelve years younger than her husband. She came from a good bourgeois family and she had pretensions to a place in Society. She was not especially pretty or cultured or even graceful. She was, in fact, averagely unattractive and certainly made no impression on men of taste and breeding. But she was emotional, oversexed and flamboyantly vivacious, so that she was incapable of being the faithful and dutiful wife of a middle-aged man.

Edmund was ideally suited to fall victim to her charms. She had only to let him know that he attracted her in order to appeal irresistibly to his Napoleonic complex. Though he had slept with tavern wenches and small-part actresses (and imagined, very probably, that they were all desperately in love with him) he had never before fascinated someone whom the world would acknowledge as a lady. That was enough to intoxicate him. In his eyes, Charlotte Cox was not a vulgar, promiscuous, rather passée temptress, but a goddess whom — unbelievably — he had captured by the impelling force of his personality. In time he supposed himself madly in love with her, just as he had once supposed himself madly in love with his wife.

But unlike Mary, Charlotte Cox had the power to hold him for as long as she willed. With the sure instincts of the harlot-manquée she understood her man. She flattered him in the subtlest way. She took pains to remind him of her own social standing, while at the same time she treated him as her adored one. She played up to all his whims and fancies, allowing him to imagine that she was, in truth, his counterpart.

In fact, her feelings for him were carnal and selfish. And his

attachment to her was merely the result of a lust for conquest.
But while *she* never regarded their affair as anything more
than a rather sordid intrigue, he at least dramatised it into something spiritual and romantic. He fooled himself, of course.
But it was only after she had left him, years later, that he
understood how hollow his love for her had been. It was only
then that he was able to write to his lawyer with savage untruth:
'... I imagine Mrs Cox's age to be about forty-five when she
first flapped her ferret-eyed affection upon me.'

Her husband, the Alderman, seemed almost as interested in
Edmund as she was herself. He used to take her to a private
box at Drury Lane on every occasion that Edmund performed;
and at the end of the play they would go round together to
his dressing room and have tea with him. Sometimes they
would invite him back to supper with them at their house in
Little Britain, and occasionally they would persuade him to
stay the night. They often used to entertain Mary as well. She
naturally liked them because of their social connections. Ironic-
ally enough, they were among Edmund's few personal friends
whom she used to invite regularly to her select dinner-parties.
Indeed, for several years the two couples were on terms of
mutual esteem and exchanged frequent cordialities.

Although Charlotte pursued Edmund almost from the
outset of their meeting, there is no proof that their actual
affair began much before 5th April, 1820, when he wrote to
her from Lynn, Norfolk:

> Dearest of Women ... I am satisfied that we were formed
> for each other; the assimilation of disposition in all its
> characters proclaims it. The theatre last night was crowded
> to excess and the applause as enthusiastic as it could be for
> the country; but Charlotte did not hear it. The neighbourhood
> of Lynn is beautiful and the walks enchanting — Charlotte
> does not partake of them ... I am satisfied we were formed
> for one another ... From the moment I saw you, I loved
> every hour; and in possession of your heart, I acknowledge
> with gratitude, that I have obtained the very summit of my
> wishes. Dear ... dear, dear girl; more than wealth, more than

life, more than heaven, I love you.

Now there is no need of Winston's diaries to tell us that before
his affair with Charlotte Edmund slept with whores as well
as any actress who was willing, and that he suffered from
recurrent venereal disease, for we knew all that from other
sources. But the affair with Charlotte was clearly overriding,
as Winston himself must have known, and he makes no reference to Edmund's sexual excesses between the time the actual
affair began, that is in the Spring of 1820, and the time it
ended about March 1824, except for the entry of 5th June that
spoke of a 'woman waiting for him'. But that 'woman' may
well have been Mrs Cox, for she came often to Drury Lane
where Edmund had a private box placed at her disposal. Indeed
in a much later entry Winston says that Elliston had placed
two private boxes at Kean's disposal — one for his wife and
the other for his 'whore' by whom he meant Mrs Cox.

As regards the previous entries about Kean's sexual excesses,
they appear to be mostly hearsay. Since Edmund's acting was
clearly bound up with his libido, I question whether he would
really have risked weakening his libido immediately before a
performance or midway through one, unless he didn't care
how he was going to do, which is inconceivable in the case of
almost any actor and certainly in the case of Kean, who had
an insatiable thirst for applause. Moreover, it would contradict
another point to be gathered from Winston's diaries. The
entry for 21st August, 1820, reads:

After the play this evening Elliston, wishing to go out of
town, proposed arrangements during his absence — particularly for Kean's nights. After some interviews with Kean,
[the latter] came into the room and said, 'Why were such
wretches brought to me?' alluding to [Mrs] West and Booth,
that the repetition of Lear would be to show them and not
Kean etc, etc, and left the room without anything being
settled.

Winston was suggesting, in other words, that Edmund couldn't abide anyone receiving any applause but himself, and was presumably speaking the truth since he was, which was seldom the case, reporting at first hand.

Edmund was still determined to go to America, notwithstanding his infatuation with Charlotte. The blandishments of Elliston — and the occasions, according to Winston, when they got drunk together — had not changed his mind. He had been forced back to Drury Lane against his will, and from a crop of new roles he had reaped only one real success. That was King Lear, and even though his performance was considered very fine by most members of the Public, it failed to win universal acclaim from the critics. It should, perhaps, be described as a vintage performance in the sense that eventually it was to rank among his greatest. Crabb Robinson wrote of it in his diary, a year later, 'He (Kean) does not need vigour or grace as Lear, but passion — and that never fails him.' But at the time it created only a mild sensation, and was judged to be far inferior to his Richard, his Overreach and his Othello. Hazlitt who, aware of the tremendous effect Garrick had made in the part, expected to be overwhelmed by Edmund's interpretation, was plainly disappointed:

> To call it a decided failure would be saying what we do not think; to call it a splendid success would be saying no less. Mr Kean did not appear to us to set his back fairly to the task or to trust implicitly to the author, but to be trying experiments upon the audience, and waiting to see the result. We never saw this daring actor want confidence before, but he seemed to cower and hesitate before the public eye in the present instance, and to be looking out for the effect of what he did, while he was doing it.

Perhaps Hazlitt was right. Perhaps Edmund had strained after applause. Perhaps, in his present nervous mood of discontent, he was incapable of 'setting his back fairly' to any task.

If this was, indeed, the outset of his affair with Charlotte, it couldn't, from his own point of view, have been better timed. What was there left for him while he was bound to a theatre where his popularity was declining, except to fall in love? He, who could not survive without adulation, fled to a woman who was prepared to give it to him unstintingly. Charlotte became 'essential' to his happiness. In her arms he found an exhilarating refuge from his wounded pride. He saw no fault in her. She had the same thoughts and feelings and tastes and impulses as he. And she worshipped him — not slavishly, of course, for she was a jealous mistress. But were not her suspicions and demands exquisitely flattering?

She gave him confidence even in his failings. For it *was* a failing, as Edmund himself knew quite well, to drink to excess and mix with whores. But she never suggested that anything he did or had done was wrong or unworthy — unless, of course, he broke an appointment with her. His extravagance and dissipation were mere vagaries excusable in a genius. She did not make him feel in the least ashamed of his associations or of his beginnings. She was all compassion and sympathy — except when his actions ran contrary to her own interests.

She liked those who were dear to him. She liked Aunt Tid and Aunt Tid liked her apparently. At any rate, Aunt Tid became a party to their affair. She was their confidante and their go-between. Edmund had to be very careful to avoid detection, and so he addressed his letters to Charlotte in the fictitious names of Mrs Alleyn, Mrs Simpson and so on, and sent them either care of Miss Tidswell or care of that other shadowy figure of his childhood, Aunt Price. One knows that Miss Tidswell hated Mary and would have grasped at any chance of taking vengeance on her. But neither did she approve of Edmund's excesses and since she was at this time still a member of the Drury Lane company, it is unlikely that Edmund would have flaunted his misbehaviour with women in front of her, as he must have done if Winston's allegations were true.

Near the end of his life she came to look after him. She was then retired and in her seventy-first year, and his doctor described her as 'tall, erect, grey-haired and exceedingly well-conducted'. The doctor asked her once, because she seemed so fond of Edmund, whether she was his mother. She answered

that she was not but that she had known him since he was a
little boy. 'And it is hard, very hard,' she added, 'to see him
fading away like this in the best part of life', and then burst
into tears.

Remorseless though her hatred of Mary was, she couldn't
have foreseen what immeasurable damage his affair with Charlotte was going to do him. As for Edmund himself, he had no
intention of sacrificing his family, which presumably was what
Aunt Tid was hoping he would do. On the other hand, Charlotte showed herself admirably suited, as Mary never was, to
be the Queen of his little tavern kingdom. R. Phillips, his
secretary, and Jack Hughes, a trusted friend who had once
been a fellow-stroller, became the organizers of her clandestine
meetings with him; and she was empowered to give them
instructions. One night, when she was sitting alone in the
stage box at Drury Lane, a Mr Crooke, who was a theatrical
agent by profession, walked in and handed her this note:

> Welcome, my life, my love, my soul, I cannot see you until
> after the farce ... How does my little darling? I introduce
> you to my friend, Mr Crooke, an officer of the Wolves,
> whom I have commissioned to be in attendance and pay
> all honour to his captain's love. I shall hurry through the
> Tobacconist as fast as possible.

Edmund secured jobs for his poor actor friends through Edward
Crooke's agency. Crooke, besides being his lieutenant in the
Wolves Club, was also a director of his charitable enterprises.
And, of course, Charlotte played up to all Edmund's 'human
feelings', his generous impulses, his hatred of 'false pride'.

> Your offer to assist poor _____ [he wrote] is noble like
> yourself — noble and unaffected — You charm me by your
> charity for I know it is not from ostentation: every day
> shoots up some unexpected tendril round the root of my
> affections ...

He was lavishly generous to her. He gave her money, clothes, a horse — anything in the world she wanted. It was all part of this highly theatrical romance about a king and his adored.

> I thank you, dear love, [he wrote] for asking for the plaid; it displays that undivided confidence which ever should subsist in hearts formed for each other. I hope my little darling will always tell me her wishes without disguise or reservations; and if love, money or industry can accomplish them, she is certain as she may be of the heart of her adorer.

What a sad, absurdly tinsel infatuation it was! At the age of thirty-one — with far more experience of the world, the seamier side of the world, than most men — he had fallen in love, as a schoolboy might, with a woman who encouraged him to romanticize her, and who played upon his vanity. He was deceived by flattery so transparent that when he tried to flatter himself in the same way he could not succeed — at least not without the aid of a great deal of brandy. She was a lady, and he made believe that he loved her passionately. But he didn't love her nearly as much as he loved fame. Not even Charlotte could alter his determination to go to America and recapture the sensational success that had been his when he first came to London.

The Drury Lane season was drawing to a close. At his benefit on 12th June, Edmund announced that he would appear in a farce called *The Admirable Crichton*, and that he would, for the first time, show a London audience some of the tricks which he had learned as a strolling player. He would dance, he would sing, he would fence — and he would be Harlequin! The great tragedian would prove how versatile an actor he really was.

'All parts' of the house were 'full in minutes', says Winston. Hazlitt arrived in a mood of amused expectancy, which was disappointed, because Edmund broke his Achilles' tendon, and therefore cried off being Harlequin.

> We do not think much of Kean's singing, [Hazlitt wrote.] We could, with a little practice and tuition, sing nearly as well

ourselves; as for his dancing, it is but *so so*, and anybody can dance; but for his jumping through a hole in the wall — clean through, head over heels, like a shot out of a culverin — 'by heavens, it would have been great!' This was fully expected at his hands, and in this expectation we were baulked.

The remainder of his audience were less gentle than Hazlitt in their sarcasm. They tittered and booed a little, and one of them remarked next day that the display would 'certainly not raise his reputation'. It certainly did not. It was an absurdly undignified publicity device which a few years before he would not have contemplated and afterwards regretted.

But now the British public had finally woken up to the fact that their 'favourite' was about to leave them. And with this awakening came a sudden realization of how much they were going to miss him. Elliston, despite loud protests from the Haymarket, that was licensed to perform straight plays during the summer, reopened Drury Lane on 15th August so that Edmund could give a series of farewell performances of all his best known characters. The final one was on 16th September when he appeared as Richard III. According to newspaper accounts, Edmund responded to 'deafening cheers' with a lengthy, grandiloquent speech. He broke down under the stress of his dramatised emotions after he'd said it might possibly be his last appearance and the audience cried, 'No, no, we hope not.' But he pulled himself together, and concluded: 'I have now to bid you farewell. My recollections will be gratifying, for they will remind me of that honourable rank in my profession to which your kindness elevated me. If at any time I have forgotten the dignity of that position, it would be imputed to the delirium which your favour inspires, and it is to you alone that I need apologize. With the deepest sentiments of esteem and gratitude, I respectfully bid you farewell.'

Winston has an entry for that day which reads:

End of play some very few persons called for Kean — intended [ie. pre planned] as I think, Kean having said to me he must address the audience if called for. He made a very poor address to them.

I suspect that this entry exemplified Winston's prejudice. Edmund may have made a 'poor address', but if it was really true that only a few people had called for him, he never would have dared speak at such length without the risk of being booed off the stage.

Before leaving London, Edmund presented Drury Lane with a plaster bust of himself, which he insisted should be placed in the principal Green Room. There was some doubt as to the propriety of this, but Elliston in his most tactful, reverential mood silenced all objections. He himself, followed by Edmund and the entire Drury Lane company in procession, carried the precious bust to the Green Room. There was a short ceremony. Elliston made a speech and Edmund made a speech. The party then settled down to a feast, with 'vast quantities' of champagne, which went on until six o'clock next morning.

Edmund went off for a short provincial tour before setting sail for America aboard the *Matilda* on 11th October. He had bade goodbye to both his wife and mistress. He was glad to be rid of Mary for a while. He knew she would be perfectly happy entertaining her grand friends, including, no doubt, the Coxes, at Clarges Street ('She has as many great friends as he has,' Susan had written, 'which I consider a greater compliment'). Nor, I suspect, was he altogether sorry to leave Charlotte. He was continually worried by the possibility of their relationship becoming public knowledge. He needed the peace of mind that could only come from being wildly enough applauded. And he thought that in America he would be assured of it.

6

One of the editors of James Winston's diaries, Alfred N. Nelson, has said that Kean is shown in them as 'a conceited braggart, a brawler, a hypochondriacal malingerer, and as a compulsive lecher'. Every one of those charges is totally disproved, so far as the evidence goes, by the year he spent in America. Not that he emerged from it unscathed. On the contrary, he was guilty at the end of so serious an error that he had to abandon his plans to extend the tour, and return home.

But at the start his hopes were surpassed. The American theatre, whose history doesn't go back much beyond the beginning of the nineteenth century, had become a rich ground for English actors, and its patrons called themselves 'a living posterity'. Edmund arrived with a ready-made reputation both as an actor and as a man to be judged by this 'living posterity'. For the past seven years, they had read in their newspapers all about his successes and his failures, his generosity and his arrogance, his courage and his weakness. Some of them were excitedly predisposed in his favour; others were intensely prejudiced against him. But they were all called upon, not to discover his genius anew, but to decide whether or not the English had overestimated his faults and his virtues.

Or so they imagined. But he showed them soon enough that he was not the kind of actor who could be judged dispassionately at first sight even by 'a living Posterity'. He had come to America for the purpose of reviving — in New York, Philadelphia, Boston and Baltimore — the historic drama of his Drury Lane debut. And that is precisely what he succeeded in doing, not because he was already known as a star, but because he still retained the power to stagger and amaze.

He returned to the glory of 1814, and the details were exactly similar. He was a centre of controversy in the Press, unreservedly admired by most critics, by a few others condemned as a cheap trickster. But members of the public, uninfluenced by critical opinion, whether disgruntled or enthusiastic, crowded to his performances, applauded him to the echo and called him 'the greatest creature they ever saw'. Once again he had audiences at his mercy. He moved like a conqueror from New York to Philadelphia, from Philadelphia to Boston, from Boston to Baltimore.

If the Americans neither increased nor diminished his fame as an actor, but merely confirmed it, at least they gave the man a chance to prove that he could thrive on success. At the outset of his London career, he had borne himself with becoming modesty. Now, as then, all those who met him testified to the charm and simplicity of his manner. They had read so much in recent years of his jealousies, his tyrannical methods, his irresponsibility and his love of ostentation that they had expected him to be a veritable ogre of unpleasantness — vain and vulgar and uncouth. They were relieved to find that he was really quite endearing. 'Kean . . . created no less surprise in the Green Room than when before the audience,' wrote W.B. Wood, director of the theatres at Philadelphia and Baltimore.

> All had heard . . . of his irregular habits, his association with the Wolf Club and other persons most likely to render his manner coarse and offensive. He appeared among us instead a mild, unassuming and cheerful man, wholly free from every affectation of superiority or dictation. His suggestions as to business on the stage were always given with indulgence, and created even in the most careless a desire to excel. His presence in the Green Room was always a source of enjoyment. I speak of him and his deportment throughout a long series of performances. In private society, particularly in the company of ladies, he was distinguished for his modest and unassuming manner as well as conversation.

He could afford to be 'indulgent' in the Green Room, for he was once more supreme in his security and beyond reach of competition. And in one respect his reception in America was more satisfying to his vanity than his London triumph had ever been. He was at last being treated as a great man. The leaders of society who crowded his dressing room, and who invited him to their dinner parties and so on had none of the cynical brilliance and class-consciousness so typical of the English aristocracy. They were as much on the defensive as Edmund was himself; and when they found that he was unaffected, 'accessible', and devoid of airs and graces, they were sincerely anxious to 'pay homage to his renown'.

Dr John Francis, who at the age of thirty, was a successful

New York practitioner, a respected philanthropist and a well-known patron of the arts, became Edmund's particular friend. No doubt, as a minor New York celebrity, he would have cut an awkward figure at Holland House. But he was well-bred, knowledgeable, and quite widely travelled. He had spent a couple of years in Europe when he was training for his profession and had received instruction from the great medical scientists of Paris, London and Edinburgh.

Dr Francis summarised what was the general feeling about Edmund when he wrote:

> He won my admiration from the moment of my first interview with him. Association and observation convinced me that he added to a mind of various culture the resources of original intellect ... the drudgery of his early life had given a pliability to his muscular powers that rendered him the most dexterous Harlequin, the most finished gentleman, the most insidious lover, the most terrific tragedian. Shakespeare was familiar to him: times, costumes, habits and other manners of his age. He had dipped into phrenology, and was a physiognomist of rare discernment ... I attribute his unrivalled success in so wide a range of characters somewhat to his extraordinary capacity for observation. He individualized every character he assumed. Wherever he was, he was all eye, all ear ... He might have been called the peripatetic philosopher.

In the company of simple men, like Dr Francis, Edmund showed off his mind and his heart at their best. 'I have given up all the frivolities of my nature ...' he wrote to Charlotte in March of 1821. And so he had. Now that he was not only revered as a great actor, but appreciated by the highest in society as a great man, he could afford to be himself and do without tavern orgies and notoriety-seeking tricks. In the words of Major Noah, editor of the New York *National Advocate*, he was a 'modest unassuming gentleman — securing the esteem of all who became acquainted with him — easy in manners — always accessible, refined and classic in conversation

— and, when animated, the very life of the festive board.'

The admiration of men of standing inevitably developed in Edmund his own inherent self-respect. He behaved with more balance and wisdom than he had ever done in his life before — or ever would again. He renounced displays. He saved his money. And he offended no one.

Of course, he got drunk occasionally. But his friends excused this weakness in him on the grounds that, while he could not resist conviviality, alcohol was poison to his constitution, which had been enfeebled by his years of suffering and near-starvation. Both Dr Francis and W.B. Wood testified to the fact that he'd be drunk on far less alcohol than the average man would be.

Edmund had found the peace of mind he sought in America. But he couldn't stay there forever. Eventually, he'd have to return to Mary and Charles, who were his responsibility; to Charlotte whom he thought he loved; and to Drury Lane, which was still his real kingdom. Perhaps Drury Lane was the most important consideration of all. He was haunted by the fear that his throne might be usurped during his absence. He wrote to Charlotte:

I hear all the adventures at Drury Lane Theatre. In your next tell me their successes, whether the humble spark of talent of the Kean still glows in the dramatic world; or if some unexpected meteor has dazzled the perception to the total extinction of the minor light. I am almost tempted to say, 'Come over and tell me all yourself', but then you could never return and I must. Besides, you would by such an act lose your rank in society which you are so well qualified to adorn . . .

He could not remain in America indefinitely — not even if Charlotte were willing to share his exile. Yet when summer came, he decided to prolong his visit by another year. He was still making 'money and fame by bushels', and he thought it would be silly to hurry away from a country where his position was unchallenged in order to return to the weary struggle of maintaining it at Drury Lane.

Towards the end of May he returned to Boston as he had promised to do, for his first visit there had been especially successful. The rush to see him had been so great that tickets had been sold by auction above their advertised price and the excess profits handed over to deserving charities. But now it was late in the season, and he had been forewarned by the management not to expect much business.

He opened on 23rd May as Lear, and the house was poor and listless. On the 24th he played Jaffier in *Venice Preserved* and the house was no better, in fact a little worse. Gone were the cheers and the giant box office receipts of only three months ago.

If he remembered that he had been warned, he would never have believed that the warning applied in his case. He was bitterly disappointed. The apathy of the Boston playgoers meant only one thing — that his popularity had dwindled and dwindled more alarmingly than it had ever done in his own country. His American dream of security was shattered. It was clear now that the public had only come to see him out of curiosity. And their curiosity was satisfied.

On Friday, 25th May, he was announced to play Richard III. At 7 o'clock, when the curtain was due to rise, he walked on to the stage in his day clothes, peeped through the curtain and saw that there were not more than twenty people in front. He had not expected a full house; but an audience of twenty for his Richard — that was too great an assault on his vanity. He informed the manager, whose name was Dickson, that he would not play. He left the theatre, and returned to the house of some 'literary friends' with whom he was spending the evening. Half an hour later, Dickson sent him an urgent message: 'Colonel Perkins and other distinguished citizens had come in', and the house was now of quite a respectable size. Dickson begged him, therefore, 'to keep faith with the public'.

But Edmund was obdurate, and Dickson was eventually obliged to explain to the audience that 'Mr Kean had positively declined to play on account of lack of patronage.'

It was lucky for him that he left Boston next morning, for

otherwise he might well have been lynched by an infuriated
mob. One newspaper called him 'an insolent pretender, an
inflated, self-conceited, unprincipled vagabond' who should
'be taken by the nose and dragged before the curtain to make
his excuses for his conduct.' There were many loyal Bostonians
only too eager to follow this advice literally for the honour of
good old Colonel Perkins and the other 'distinguished citizens'
who had been insulted by the hoity-toity little *English* play-
actor.

The outcry swiftly became national. The newspapers of New
York, Philadelphia and Baltimore let fly at Edmund with a
violence of language that made the attacks launched against
him in his own country appear mild by comparison. He was
himself overwhelmed by the onslaught, for he could not see
how he had offended so grossly by refusing to play before a
slender audience in Boston. He wrote to Dickson:

> I much regret the occasion of my abrupt departure, but you
> must feel with me that my professional reputation must not
> be trifled with ... a total desertion of the public to that
> character, which has been the foundation of my fame and
> fortune, requires a greater portion of philosophy than I am
> master of ...

That was the candid truth, which he later elaborated in a
long letter to the *National Advocate*. But the truth, as usual,
did him far more harm than good. The American people had
refused to believe those stories to his discredit which had
appeared in the English newspapers. Now it appeared that he
had come among them a mountebank in gentleman's clothing;
and the fact that they had been deceived, had thought him
'modest' and 'unassuming' accentuated their fury. His letter
in the *National Advocate* only added fuel to the flames that
were burning away the last vestiges of his popularity.

He soon realised for himself that there would be no use
his accepting further engagements. Instead of trying to set
matters right by offering a suitably grovelling apology, he
announced that, though unrepentant, he had decided to leave

the United States immediately.

He spent his last day in New York (4th June, 1821) with Dr Francis, who had remained loyal to him. Some months before he had become obsessed with the idea of erecting in the churchyard of St Paul's a monument to George Frederick Cooke, a famous actor who had exhausted the patience of the English public by his flagrant errancy and had spent the last year of his life (1810–1811) in America as a virtual outcast. He was rather like Kean as an actor, and like him, at least superficially, as a man. It was no wonder that Edmund protested passionately that Cooke was the greatest actor who ever lived. And no wonder he longed for his memory to be respected. Unconsciously, he must have known that in honouring Cooke, he was paying tribute to himself.

On 4th June, the work of erecting Cooke's monument was complete. In the afternoon, Edmund went with Dr Francis

> to pay his last devotion to it . . . Tears fell from his eyes in abundance, and as the evening closed he walked Broadway, listened to the chimes of Trinity, returned again to the churchyard and sang sweeter than ever 'Those Evening Bells' and 'Come o'er the Sea'. Dr Francis, who played the part of a silent observer 'fancied that he saw a child of genius . . . deprived of the solace which the world cannot give, the sympathies of the heart'.

Next morning Edmund began his journey homewards. By one impulsive act of folly he had ruined what would otherwise have been the happiest and most rewarding year of his life.

7

No evidence has yet been discovered about Edmund's behaviour on the voyage home. But it is certain that he arrived back in Liverpool on 20th July tired, dispirited and far from well.

However, the reception that Elliston had arranged for him

must have cheered him up — at any rate for the time being. It was the kind of reception fitted for a King returned to his Kingdom after a lengthy absence abroad. Elliston had ordered 'huge notices' to be plastered all over the town announcing that Edmund would arrive at Drury Lane about noon on Monday 23rd July and that he would positively reappear that night in the character of Richard III. In Winston's diary the entry for 23rd July tells rather tersely what further preparation Elliston, the master showman, had made for his star's triumphal return.

At twelve o'clock a courier announced Kean was coming. In about three minutes the cavalcade arrived. They came by the pit door to the stage door — six outriders, Mr Elliston's carriage and four [greys], himself only in it; then a post chaise and four [blacks], Russell, Hughes and Kean in it; post chaise, Cooper in its mob. All the people in the theatre assembled at the door including fifty soldiers and gave him three cheers as he arrived and again on the stage.

A more vivid account of the triumphal procession to Drury Lane was given in a newspaper:

Six outriders, in a medley of costumes of all nations of the earth that do not go absolutely tattooed, constituted the vanguard; then came Elliston himself in solitary grandeur in his own carriage drawn by four greys. The hero of the Triumph next — Kean himself, likewise in his carriage, supported by Russell and Hughes in cocked hats, drawn by four blacks. John Cooper, in the simple majesty of his undecorated form, followed drawn also by four . . . piebald. A troop of horsemen formed the flank, composed of bruisers, the whole was brought up by the heterogeneous rabble which the progressive affair had from pillar to post enlisted.

This charade was followed by an official reception and a formal dinner party presided over by the Great Lessee and attended by the entire *corps dramatique*. Elliston, of course, had his tongue in his cheek, but he knew how well Edmund would respond to these tinsel celebrations.

And for a brief while Edmund did respond to them magnificently. He played Richard III before a packed audience, and they greeted his performance with such cheering as 'had never been heard before'. The house was again crowded for his Shylock on 25th July and again on 26th July for his Othello. But he was very hoarse, and on 27th July Elliston was obliged to print a doctor's certificate instead of a playbill. It read ominously:

> Mr Kean is very unwell this morning, and the medicine which I think needful for his recovery will not have completed my intent before late in the evening of tomorrow. I, therefore, think it most prudent to put off his acting until Monday; indeed, he might not be capable tomorrow and if called upon might be laid up for many days afterwards. [signed] Ant. Carlisle.

He did reappear on Monday, 30th July, as Richard III; according to Winston, 'after much persuasion'. But he declined to play again during the specially extended season, and left London to spend the rest of the summer in the provinces.

There is no evidence of exactly when he was able to see Charlotte. But on 16th August he wrote to her from Swansea saying that Mary had come across a part of one of her letters to him, and there had been a 'terrible explosion'. Mary had made him swear that he would never see his mistress again, and she herself intended to cut off all relations with the Coxes. Meanwhile she insisted that she and Charles had the right to accompany him wherever he went. She was continually suspicious, for she knew well enough that he was not to be trusted.

> The eyes of Argus may be eluded [he wrote from his next stop] but those of a jealous wife impossible. Even now I am on tenterhooks. I expect the door forced open and 'What are you writing?' the exclamation, or Susan to see if everything is comfortable, or Charles with a handful of endearments

for his dear papa, all tending to the same thing 'what is he about?'

A little later he wrote from Carlisle:

... she left me yesterday for London; if that had not been the case I could not have written to you now. I am watched more closely than Bonaparte, independent of which I have never been more than three days in a place ...

There were many such outbursts of resentment against his wife, which vulgarly he confided to his mistress. But then he had come to resent the former, while he was romantically in love with the latter. And Mary, for her part, wouldn't have minded about his affair, if she hadn't thought that her own future was threatened by it. He might run off with Charlotte. Then what would happen to all the trappings of gentility that he had given her?

Yet he knew that he would never, under any circumstances, desert his family. If Aunt Tid had tried in vain to make him see how ill-suited Mary was to be his wife, Charlotte would never be able to wrench him free of her. For he had a son, and though he had no bond of true sympathy with Charles, he was a proud and, in his way, a conscientious father. Charles was being educated as a gentleman, just as Edmund had always intended. He was a preparatory schoolboy now and would soon be going to Eton. Edmund was determined that his son should never become an actor. He flew into a passion once when Mary suggested, in her fond, motherly way, that dear Charles had leanings towards the stage and was already very gifted.

But while he found no pleasure in Mary's company, his mistress had the power to comfort him in his blackest moments. He wrote to her from Bath:

... In this infernal city my endeavours are totally failing ... My mind wants my own dear darling to console with. My fevered head wants rest in the bosom of my Charlotte.

He carried on his intrigue in a furtive, secretive way which stripped it of any romantic semblance and made it appear far more sordid and dishonourable than it actually was. His precautions were elaborate. Just before his return to London from Sussex in November 1821, he wrote to Charlotte:

> ... On no account come near the park. I shall cross over Waterloo Bridge on Tuesday between 1 and 2 o'clock. I will see you on Wednesday in the saloon of the theatre. I have declared you are in the West Indies. If you are seen I am ruined.

Of course, there was the Alderman to be considered as well. But he was proving either very complaisant or extraordinarily blind. Though Mary refused to see the Coxes, the Alderman continued to allow Edmund every facility to consort with his wife. Though he was no longer welcome at Clarges Street, he went on inviting Edmund to his own home in Wellington Street, as if there had been no change at all in their good relationship. Indeed, Edmund had the run of the Coxes' house unknown to Mary. Sometimes he would arrive dead drunk in the middle of the night, and would be given a room to sleep in.

The Alderman never tried to keep Charlotte away from her lover. On the contrary, when he was unable to take her to Drury Lane himself, he sent her there with his niece, Anne Wickstead. On one occasion they all four of them drove off to Croydon together late at night. Next morning the Alderman returned to London 'to settle some business', cheerfully leaving his wife in Edmund's tender charge.

In August, 1822, when Edmund was touring the provinces without much success, he had a sudden yearning for Charlotte's society. He begged her to meet him in Birmingham. 'Meet me as soon as possible ...' he wrote, 'that is as soon as safety will permit.' She came to Birmingham at once. She assured the anxious Edmund that she had fobbed her husband off with the plausible story that she was going to visit her mother in Brighton. But this time the Alderman was not so easily gulled. He sent off his son by a former marriage, Robert Cox, in hot pursuit, and Robert found the lovers in *flagrante delicto*. Charlotte returned with him to London, leaving Edmund behind in a blue funk.

In desperation he turned to Aunt Tid. 'L.B.,' he wrote (he called Charlotte L.B., which stood for little breeches, because once at Drury Lane she had dressed herself in his costume):

> L.B. will explain the perplexities we are in and I have so much confidence in you that I am sure you will render us the utmost assistance. I place her for a time under your protection. Her impudence is great but her affection is unbounded. To your charge I trust her till affairs are accommodated. She has plenty of money and I will rather add to your comforts than diminish them. Your affectionate friend and nephew, Edmund Kean.

But nothing happened. The Alderman neither showed Charlotte the door nor even scolded her. Had Robert Cox held his tongue? Or had the Alderman, in his liberality, decided to ignore the incident? Edmund merely heaved a great sigh of relief. The danger was past.

In a sense he was glad of the Alderman's existence, for it gave him the chance to impress upon Charlotte the absolute necessity for secrecy. She was getting increasingly restless. She had wanted to go to America with him, and she was no longer satisfied with passionate love letters, with clandestine meetings, with money and presents galore. She was demanding recognition. She wished the world to know of her association with the great actor. It is likely she hoped in the end to marry him.

Edmund found it difficult to resist Charlotte's demands and to protest that he was 'all in all hers forever.' But her husband provided him with his best defence against her accusations of timidity. He was the 'great cause' why Edmund could not do as his mistress willed. 'Let but the great cause be removed,' he wrote shortly after the Birmingham scare, 'and I shall laugh at all agencies though they may pursue me in chaise and four; in other words let him but go abroad and I will dare the worst.'

And a while later '. . . Could the great cause be removed . . . I would hold my little darling to my heart and sleep in spite of thunder.'

Charlotte had very much less respect for the 'great cause' than Edmund had. She was becoming very indiscreet.

In January 1823 a party was made up to spend a week at Salisbury. Aunt Tid and Anne Wickstead went by post-chaise. Mr and Mrs Cox travelled with Edmund in his coach. The week passed happily enough. But on the last night Charlotte behaved so obviously that the Alderman, out of self-respect, could no longer ignore the truth. He made a scene. He threatened a duel. And there was some talk of 'pistols being produced'.

Next morning Edmund paid all the expenses of the party and in addition lent Cox £10 for his fare back to London. But he was not sure the quarrel had been patched up, and he wrote Cox this foolish letter:

> My dear Cox, I have seriously been considering the mass of nonsense uttered by us two last night at Salisbury . . . I must be the worst of villains, if I could take the man by the hand, while meditating towards him an act of injustice. You do not know me, Cox; mine are follies, not vices. It has been my text to do all the good I could in the world, and when I am called to a superior bourne, my memory may be blamed but not despised . . .

At the same time he wrote to Charlotte:

> Your incaution has been very near bringing our acquaintance to the most lamentable crisis. Of course, he will show you the letter I have written him; appear to countenance it, and let him think we are never to meet again and in doing so he has lost a friend.

Cox took no immediate action; and though Edmund steered clear of him from then on, he believed he had avoided the Alderman's vengeance and was free to carry on his intrigue unsuspected. It is very doubtful, however, that Charlotte obeyed his instructions to 'appear to countenance' his letter to her husband, for she became more troublesome than ever. She began to insist on his sacrificing his family. When he was in London towards the end of the year she presented him with some kind of ultimatum. On 9th December (1823) he wrote to her:

What can I say? I love you better than all the world — all beyond. I see no remedy for our disease but patience, and that must be exerted to the utmost. On my return from America [he was planning a second visit] all shall be as you wish, till then it is impossible. You must think for a man struggling to obtain competence for his family, which the circumstances of our connection must utterly destroy. I feel for you most sincerely, on my soul, my heart is breaking, but any rash step would destroy our hopes forever. I long to see you but will not come to your house. If you enter the front door Theatre Royal Drury Lane, I will meet you thro' the other . . .

But Charlotte would not give in. She was weary of Edmund's hesitancy and secretiveness. She embarked on an affair with a man called Whatmore, who worked as a clerk in her own house. Evidently she wished Edmund to find out about it.

In January, he wrote her this pathetic letter:

My dear love, I wrote angrily to you yesterday, forgive me, I was disappointed at not receiving a letter from you and wrote in irritation. Indeed, love, I would not doubt you for worlds; for I live but thinking of you, and if I lose you I am sure my heart will break.

Mr FitzSimons says that their final meeting was in Regent's Park when she gave him a tongue-lashing, and in the course of it told him of her affair with Whatmore who, she said, was younger, better-looking and far more virile than he. FitzSimons indulges in a considerable amount of doubtful detail here, though not so much as his source, Willson Disher, the author of

a 'fictional' biography of Edmund Kean. But if the substance
of the Disher-FitzSimons story is true, one can readily understand why the tender feelings that Edmund had once had for
Charlotte should have turned to bitter contempt even before
the Alderman discovered that his wife was sleeping with his
clerk. That was in March 1824. The Alderman walked out of
his home swearing that he 'would never again live under the
same roof as that woman whose perfidy he had detected'.

A few days later Charlotte left the house with Anne Wickstead to seek quarters of her own. The Alderman returned,
and it was then that he discovered all of Edmund's love letters
'carefully, but most unaccountably left packed up'. He at
once consulted a solicitor and began proceedings to sue his
false friend for criminal conversation with his wife.

Winston's diary for 30th June reads:

> Robins said this day he had seen sixty-eight letters in Amory's
> (Cox's solicitor) from Kean to Mrs Cox. They were such as
> would damn him in the public opinion. Kean's solicitor
> proposed to let judgement go by default and refer damages to
> sheriff's court, but Cox's solicitor would not agree to give up
> the letters. One of them, it seems, proves that he, Kean, slept
> with two whores and sent them at eleven at night to abuse
> Mrs Cox, of whom he was jealous of a Mr W[hatmore].

But apart from Winston's diaries — and this may be suggestive
of their reliability — there is no evidence at all that such a letter
was ever written or that Kean slept with two prostitutes whom
he sent round afterwards to be abusive to Mrs Cox. Indeed, if
anything of the sort actually happened, it is extraordinary that
no mention of it was made at the trial when every letter that
Kean ever wrote to Mrs Cox was read out for the delectation of
the spectators and seized on afterwards by the multitude of
Kean's detractors. Just the same the fact that Charlotte left
those letters where the Alderman was bound to find them
indicated that she wanted vengeance on him. Nor could she
have hit on a more certain way of getting it.

Incidentally, neither FitzSimons nor Disher makes use of

Kean's attempt at exculpation which appears in Winston's diary under the date of 7th April, 1824:

> Cox got into room, although ordered not to be admitted, and was persuaded to leave the room, and it appears from Kean's story to me next day (when he took out two pistols and told me he carried them to shoot Cox if he attacked him) that it was well-known he intrigued with Cox's wife, a younger woman than Cox, who has an annuity and [that] Kean had contributed to the support of Mr and Mrs Cox. She, Mrs Cox, had lately confessed to Kean that she was not constant to him but was intimate with another man — Whatmore ... All this came to Cox's ears, who pretended, he has just known of her inconstancy, and [he] vowed vengence* against Kean.

While his affair with Charlotte Cox was in progress, Edmund's professional life was giving him little satisfaction. In November, he returned to Drury Lane for the 1821 season, and found himself worse off than he had been before his American venture. Nothing new that he attempted caused the faintest stir, and even in his famous characters he wasn't much of a draw. The public were taking him for granted again.

He was so tired in spirit at the age of thirty-three that half of him yearned to withdraw from public life. He'd found his St Helena in the Isle of Bute, off the west coast of Scotland. Bute was many miles from Drury Lane. But it was within easy distance of Glasgow and Greenock, and he was often able to go there for a few days' rest between provincial engagements. Apart from Rothesay, its capital, a busy industrial town which could be quickly left behind on foot, the island appeared almost deserted. Edmund had been shown its secrets by Duncan M'Corkindale, landlord of the Bute Arms at Rothesay. And a little while afterwards he had bought 24 acres of land overlooking 'Sweet Loch Fad'. A house was built to his order on the site; he looked forward to the day when he would settle down in it for good with his wife and family. Or so he made himself believe.

*   Sic.

Mary could not understand what crazy impulse had prompted him to purchase a property which was completely cut off from the world — unless it had been a desire to get rid of her while he pursued his intrigue with his mistress. She expressed her view, years later, in a letter to Barry Cornwall:

> ... We took 22 acres of land from Lord Bute's factor — Lord Bute's property — as sterile — as forlorn — as desolate — as you can imagine — built and furnished a house in a spot where there was no ... creature within three miles of the place. We paid pounds for what was not worth shillings ... it was a madness done by the desire of Mrs Cox to hide me and ended in utter ruin to us all ...

But Mary was always a dangerously prejudiced historian. In this case her word is refutable by direct evidence. The property at Bute still exists much as Edmund left it, and anyone who cares to make the pilgrimage will understand why he called it, exuberantly, 'his island paradise'. His love for it had nothing whatever to do with Charlotte Cox.

The 1822 Drury Lane season started without Edmund; he was fulfilling engagements in Scotland and supervising the building of his Bute house. Elliston, meanwhile, after the financial disaster he had suffered last season as a result of Kean's comparative failure, had decided drastic measures were necessary. Among them, he had persuaded Charles Mayne Young, Kemble's Covent Garden successor, to join the Drury Lane Company as a star tragedian. Edmund was furious when he heard what had happened; he wrote to Elliston from Dundee on 13th October:

> ... I find Mr Young ... is engaged for thirty nights and that my services are wanted to act with him — now this I call exceedingly impudent ... the throne is mine. I will maintain it — even at the expense of expatriation — go where I will I shall always bear it with me — and even if I sailed to another part of the globe, no man in this profession can rob me of the character of the first English actor ...

Edmund's indignation was allied with fear. Charles Mayne
Young had natural attributes which appealed to the public —
dignity, good looks and a melodious voice. He had one advan-
tage to make Edmund feel vastly inferior to him. He was a
gentleman. His father had been a fashionable London doctor,
and he himself had been educated at Eton.

Just the same, Edmund might have been as confident of
vanquishing Young as he had been of defeating Booth five
years ago, if his health had not deteriorated badly since then.
He had no longer such reserves of strength. He dreaded comparison with Young chiefly because he could not be certain of
summoning enough energy to match the importance of an
occasion.

On 23rd October, he wrote from Rothesay — his house on
the island was not yet completed — a second pathetically
moving appeal to Elliston:

> ... You must forgive me being jealous of my hard-earned
> laurels ... Mr Young has many advantages that I have not —
> a commanding figure, sonorous voice — & above all Lordly
> connection ... all I ask of you is to let me retire with my
> reputation undiminished ... as the Covent Garden Hero —
> comes upon my ground as the Challenger — I have doubt-
> less my choice of weapons, he *must* play Iago! — before I
> act Jaffier I am told he is extraordinary great in Pierre —
> if so — I am beaten — this must not be — I cannot bear it —
> I would rather go in chains to Botony Bay — I am not ashamed
> to say I am afraid of the contest ...

But it was part of the paradox of Edmund's character that
however greatly he feared an event he invariably faced up to it
boldly in the end. A large, excited audience came to see him
fight the second biggest battle of his career, and inevitably he
responded to their expectancy. He did not, to be sure, treat
Young as murderously as he had treated Booth. But he more
than held his own. He gave a very fine performance which was
greeted with louder applause than he had heard for a long while.
And when it was over the audience were satisfied that while

Young was certainly a good actor, Edmund was still supreme.

This meant that Elliston had merely to announce the names of his rival tragedians on the same bill to be certain of record box-office returns. He made them play together continually, not only in *Othello* but in other plays, such as *Venice Preserved* and *Cymbeline*, where there were two parts of equivalent importance. The crowds returned to Drury Lane. Popular excitement over Edmund was again at fever pitch, and Young, too, had his partisans. Nowadays it is hard to understand the lust which the public had 150 years ago for histrionic fisticuffs.

At the end of the season Elliston had made a handsome profit, which he needed badly. But Young declined to renew his contract. He complained that he had been fouled by Edmund, and alleged that the latter had made use of all the vulgar tricks of a thoroughly selfish actor. He had, for example, invariably stood a few paces upstage of his fellow players. No doubt Young's complaints were perfectly justified. Winston's diary on 11th November says 'Kean returned to Drury Lane but appeared to be very sulky all the evening . . . He dressed in second Green Room.' His determination to stay on top by whatever means, was, as I have said, understandable, but he evidently disliked Young personally. Winston says in a later entry that he remarked angrily, 'I have to play again with that bloody thundering bugger.'

Elliston engaged Macready for the following season as a replacement for Young, and thus looked forward to another battle between star tragedians. But Edmund had retreated to Bute under cover of a doctor's certificate. On 18th November (1823) he wrote to his secretary, Phillips, at Drury Lane:

I must differ with you, about my coming to London. Fabius Maximus conquered not by fighting a powerful enemy, but by avoiding him . . .

I shall not move from this heavenly spot, till Caius Gracchus meets his fate . . . The Christmas pantomime over — and a general stagnation of public excitement; and *then* — like a hawk I'll pounce upon my prey. Write and send bills, or those penny *critiques*, every day!!!

Though Edmund waited in vain for the downfall of his new rival, Macready took a three months' leave of absence at the beginning of December and simultaneously Edmund returned to Drury Lane. When Macready came back in the middle of April, Edmund immediately scurried off into the provinces. On 10th May he was actually billed to play Richard III, and his appearance with Macready would have been bound to follow, but he provided another medical certificate stating that he had been taken seriously ill at Derby and was unable to move. On 15th May, he wrote to Alfred Bunn, Elliston's manager, saying that he would not play with Macready and that he'd been ordered to Brighton for his health. Dunn, the Drury Lane Treasurer, went to Brighton and learned that Edmund was staying at the Regent Hotel. He was refused admittance to Edmund's presence, but he finally saw Mary, and through her conveyed a note to Edmund which contained Elliston's compliments together with a gentle enquiry after the invalid's health!

Edmund was furious.

I hate a trickster, [he wrote to Elliston]. You have employed unworthy means to disturb me in my solitude ... You have pursued me by a trick, and I should deign you no reply; but I am here, Sir, under the direction of Sir Anthony Carlisle, and will not stir from this place until I have gone through all the routine of medicine and sea-bathing, prescribed by that great man ... If I am pursued either by trick or openly, I shall retire to La Belle France for some weeks ...

I leave you in no distress. You have Macready; Macready Elliston! — why should you be anxious about poor Kean? Yet a breath — a breath, I say, of Kean shall confound a generation of Youngs and Macreadys.

On 21st May, before Elliston had an opportunity to answer him, he fulfilled his threat of retiring to *La Belle France*. By then the thing that he had tried so hard to conceal for so long was already public knowledge. In fact, at the beginning of

April, Cox had created a scene outside an hotel where Edmund was presiding at a public dinner. He brandished a pistol and threatened to shoot the man who had wronged him. Edmund wasn't nearly so worried by the prospect of the trial, now that it was unavoidable, as he was by immediate theatre politics. After all, Charlotte was so obviously a bitch. In exasperation he had often called her so in the days when he had loved her. Now he hated her and called her a bitch in good earnest, and a whore as well. As for the Alderman — he was a liar and a cheat. No jury on earth composed of decent men would exalt the Coxes at his expense.

Mary, because she no longer had anything to fear from Mrs Cox, was quite content to accompany him on his journey to *La Belle France*. On 21st May, he wrote to his friend, Jack Hughes:

> . . . The closer they pursue the further I shall recede — by the time you receive this Mrs Kean and myself are on our way to Paris — where I shall remain till I see the last night advertised at Drury Lane Theatre. Settle all bills for me; I will discharge them on the instant I return — I shall then quit England for *ever* — but I carry with me the reputation of the first English actor, which if I had allowed them to have their way, I could not have done, if I had acted — I know hundreds were prepared for hostility, and in the bad parts they were forcing me to play with Macready he must have skimmed the cream of my professional dish. — he may now take the whole, — & the public may talk and be damned I shall soon be out of hearing . . . I was so ill, if I had attempted to act I am convinced I shou'd have fallen on the stage. — Dunn was sent to Brighton & I immediately got into the Packet & sailed — I shall not act now, till August — my *Dublin engagement* and then — *Vale Patria*.

It is strange that Edmund should have sought peace in the company of the person who was least able to understand him and most likely to irritate him. Possibly she insisted on being with him, but seventeen years of marriage had taught her no tact in dealing with her husband. In Paris the Keans were lavishly entertained by Talma, the great French tragedian. Mary treated him with that same wilting reverence with which she had once captured Edmund's heart. 'The last time Talma came to the hotel to us,' she told Barry Cornwall, 'seeing me so delighted with his acting promised to act all his great characters for me but Mr Kean hurried off and I lost a great treat.'

Was she really surprised that Edmund 'hurried off'? He, who fled from England, because he had been unable to bear the thought of the public's applause for Macready, was hardly likely to relish his own wife's adulation of a rival actor. He took her back to England via Boulogne.

On 20th August, while Edmund was fulfilling provincial engagements in Ireland, Mary and Susan and Charles travelled by carriage north to Bute, where his house, called Woodend, was ready for occupation. Mary wept most of the way up. Even after she arrived, she remained obstinately inconsolable. She hated Bute and she derived no pleasure from her duties as the wife of an estate owner. Susan agreed with her 'that it was preposterous to think that a man as gay as Edmund would always be content to remain in Bute', but at the same time she understood the fascination of the place. '. . . To say it is beautiful,' she wrote to Margaret Roberts, 'is not in my mind saying enough — it is perfectly enchanting, but so lonely one almost startles at the sound of their own voices — but its loneliness is no imperfection to me, indeed it gives me the idea that all nature was in repose — so very sweet and tranquil is all around . . .'

Susan wrote this letter in December, when she was living alone at Woodend, for Charles had returned to spend his second half at Eton and Mary had gone to meet her husband in Glasgow. But she was quite content to be left behind. She liked running the house and looking after the gardener, who was paid twenty-five shillings per week, and the six labourers, who were paid one shilling and six pence per day. Edmund had sent her a parrot to keep her company.

She was very interested in all the improvements that he intended to carry out later. He said that soon they would be able to live free, for he would get fish from the loch and would shoot rabbits and hares (he had already shot two hares). 'When Edmund returns,' she wrote, 'he is to bring a low four-wheeled carriage such as I can drive in his absence. I am to buy a cow in the Spring when we shall have cream and butter of our own.'

But even Susan seemed to realize on what very rickety foundations Edmund's plans and enthusiasms were based. For the trial between the Alderman and himself was now fixed for 15th January, and 'Heaven only knew what the end of it would be.'

The Kean family spent Christmas together in Scotland. But it was not a very happy celebration. Nerves were at breaking point; and a few days later there was a first-class row between Edmund and Mary. The servants on the estate never forgot how the coachman came down from the house with an order from Mary 'to yoke the horses' and how Edmund shouted after him, 'There must be no carriage yoked here without my orders.' The precise cause of the quarrel may only be guessed at; perhaps it had something to do with Mary's desire to return to London. But its consequence was that Mary stayed behind in Bute, while Edmund went to London to face his trial alone.

He was blind to its dangers, though his solicitor had warned him about how bad a light the letters would put him in. He was convinced that he would win the case. He had ordered his dresser at Drury Lane to get in a quantity of brandy, so that on the night of 15th January he would be able to drink with his friends to the damnation of 'all whores and lying Aldermen'.

8

For months before there had been paragraphs in the Press about the sensational letters that Cox had discovered. Thomas Creevey, the diarist, had written to his step-daughter, Elizabeth Ord ... 'another *slip* is Mrs Alderman C — with our tragedian Kean. He has been at his letters too, one of which to the lady was intercepted by the alderman and began, "You dear impu-

Kean as Hamlet.

Robert William Elliston.

dent little Bitch" — Can anything be more soft and romantic?'

Though they were, in fact, the letters of a man romantically in love, they were also sprinkled with reminders of his gutter-bred beginnings, some of which were considered unfit for newspapers to print. Nor was Edmund respectful enough of Charlotte's supposedly hitherto unblemished virtue and her 'rank in society' to conceal from her that he had venereal disease which was recurrent. 'By the bye,' he wrote to her on one occasion, "I am ashamed to say I am very ill, therefore it is fortunate you are not near me***" (the asterisks conceal words that were found to be unprintable).

Edmund boasted that he was going to 'turn his accusers to infamy and contempt'. If he really believed that, he cannot have realized how eager a large section of the Press was to punish him for his arrogance and effrontery — for the fact that he wasn't, despite his pretensions, a gentleman. And he cannot have understood what a golden opportunity his letters had given them. They spelt death to Edmund's hopes of escaping disaster. Of course, they established his adultery, but far worse than this they seemed to show his perfidy, his deceit and his indecent vulgarity. To have explained them away he would have had to lay bare the inner workings of his soul. And unfortunately the soul is not evidence in law.

The trial was held on 17th January, 1825, before the Lord Chief Justice. The Common serjeant appeared for the plaintiff. Mr Scarlett was leading counsel for the defence. The court was packed to suffocation. A few of Edmund's friends were present, and Elliston turned up to support him. But the leaders of fashion, the shorthand Press writers and the noisy idlers who made up the rest of the throng were there to laugh, jeer, gloat and get hysterical pleasure from the public exposure of a man whose conduct they had for years resented.

Mr Scarlett did not attempt to excuse his client's conduct. But he suggested first that Mrs Cox was a wanton and secondly that the Alderman had condoned her infidelity with Mr Kean. For these reasons he urged the jury to decide that the plaintiff far from being entitled to the £2000 he had claimed should not get more than a farthing's damages.

In his summing up the Lord Chief Justice ruled that the affair with Whatmore was irrelevant to the issue, and that the allegation that Mrs Cox had had two affairs previous to her meeting with Kean was unproved. He also said there was no reason to suppose that the plaintiff had actually been aware of his wife's infidelity.

At the same time, he pointed out that the Alderman's behaviour had been very far from that of a devoted husband, and he urged the jury to take this fact into consideration when they came to assess the damages. After a few minutes of whispered conversation the jury brought in a verdict for the plaintiff and awarded him £800.

The case of *Cox v. Kean* was over, but the sequel followed with such thoroughness and immediacy that it might almost have been rehearsed in advance. Verbatim reports of the trial appeared in all the newspapers. Indecent songs, ballads, playlets and caricatures dealing with Edmund and his mistress sold like hot cakes. A pamphlet entitled *Secrets Worth Knowing*, which was a pornographic forgery of Charlotte's 'suppressed' letters to her lover, was rushed through the Press by an enterprising publisher. And in spite of the growing plethora of information — real and concocted — a Sunday newspaper advertised widely in advance: '*Cox v. Kean* — Verbatim report of this trial *with all* the letters, tragical and comical, will be given gratis in a supplement . . .'

Though the Coxes won no sympathy, the *Times* led a ferocious campaign against Edmund. Its report of the trial next morning occupied most of its space (advertisements aside, ten columns out of a total of just over thirteen). The report included all the spicier letters; and though still fuller reports were to be published subsequently in pamphlet form, the *Times'* account was never to be deprived of one unique distinction — the printing of the word 'bitch' in full. This breach of editorial decorum was presumably meant to be interpreted as a case of the end justifying the means, for simultaneously the *Times* launched an editorial campaign to force Kean into temporary retirement. It described him as being 'advanced many steps in profligacy beyond the most profligate of his sisters and brethren of the stage', and continued: 'It is of little consequence whether the character of King Richard III or Othello be well or ill acted; but it is of importance that public feeling be not shocked, and public decency be not outraged.'

That particular importance had not apparently occurred to the rest of the Press, which, by comparison, was slow to recognize an outrage to public decency when it saw it and whose immediate reaction to the trial was far less violent and obsessive. But the *Times* had the power to set the pace, and within a day or two the story of Kean's adultery became depicted as a major national scandal. Virtually every newspaper and periodical treated the issue raised by the *Times* as though it were the burning question of the hour. Most, though not quite all of them, tried to outdo each other in their protestations of moral outrage. Thus the *Sunday Monitor*, as soon as its chance came, said that the story of Kean's adultery was so vile that 'Happily no parallel' to it could be 'found in ancient or modern times.'

Edmund was due to give a series of performances at Drury Lane – the first of them on 24th January. As the Press campaign against him gathered momentum, the guardians of law and order took fright, and a message was sent from the Home Secretary (Peel) to Elliston, strongly urging a postponement of the engagement on the grounds that there might otherwise be grave public disturbances. Elliston said that he would have to leave the matter up to Mr Kean and Mr Kean refused to comply.

The following entries in Winston's diary given an idea of where his sympathies lay:

January 22nd – Sir Richard Birnie said today that the Secretary of State [Robert Peel] had advised so obnoxious a character as Kean had better not appear so soon after the trial.

January 23rd: Mr Elliston went to Kean at the Greyhound, Croydon, but he had left the previous night. On the Monday morning Kean sent for Mr Elliston [to come to Miss] Tidswell's lodging, where he was in bed. The apology was sent him for his inspection. Hughes came shortly after and said he and Sigel*

---

*   Sic.

went down on Saturday, stayed with [him] about an hour
and a half, then left, he having ordered his night candlestick
to go to bed, saying he should get jollily drunk on Sunday,
come to town on Monday morning, and be ready for Monday
evening to act. However, he changed his mind and, at two in
the morning, ordered a chaise, came to town on the Sunday.
He got drunk as he proposed and on Monday had his dinner
in his room at half past four with Gattie [?] and others of
the same class.*

In its issue of 21st January, the *Times* had come near to
advocating a lynching. It called Kean an adulterer 'whose
offence' was 'aggravated by the most shocking circumstances
of indecency, perfidy, brutality, obscenity, and hypocrisy'.
It said that this man 'to show himself before the public with
all the disgrace of guilt round his neck' would be 'as great an
outrage to decency, as if he were to walk naked through the
streets at mid-day'. And it predicted that Drury Lane would
be crowded 'with all the numerous class of morbidly curious
idlers who flock to a play or an execution to see how a man
looks when he is hanged or deserves to be hanged.'

The *Times* got what it had asked for. The audience that
jammed the vast auditorium of Drury Lane on the night of
24th January, 1825 included very few playgoers who had
come to see a great actor in one of his greatest parts. For the
most part, it was a mob of demonstrators, with a minority
of counter-demonstrators recruited from Kean's tavern kingdom. It included bruisers, prostitutes, young bloods with
hunting horns to blow, white-haired members of the Society
for the Suppression of Vice with propaganda placards to raise
on high, drunkards, thieves and an amorphous collection of
sensation-seekers. Collectively, it had come to stage its own
show, not to watch another's; and if the result hadn't quite
the sadistic attraction of a public execution, it was a match
for any bear-baiting spectacle.

The demonstrators greeted Edmund on his entrance with a
great prurient yell, like the cry of some barbarian army scent-
ing rape. They pelted him with orange peel and rotten eggs;
they jeered and hooted at him; screamed out obscenities;

*   i.e. prostitutes.

bellowed 'Heart-Strings', 'Little Breeches' and 'Go Back to Mother Cox' — roared with cruel laughter at their own cruel sallies. The counter-demonstrators fought back with shouts of 'Down with the *Times*' and 'Down with Cant', but they only succeeded in swelling the general clamour, which never for a moment subsided while Edmund was on the stage, so that his whole performance might as well have been given in dumb show. At the end, he stood before his persecutors, 'the proud representative of Shakespeare's heroes', as he liked to call himself, mutely appealing for a chance to speak, until a further shower of missiles drove him out of sight, though not into submission.

Next morning, a sheet, called the *Theatrical Observer*, described the counter-demonstrators as 'wretches' and the demonstrators as men who 'loving their country's reputation and feeling the blessings of a virtuous and happy fire-side, had mustered in a good cause'. Significantly, however, the paper added that the 'good cause' was now sufficiently prosecuted and that when Kean gave his next performance the 'task of chastisement' should be dropped.

Not even the *Times* had dared be logical enough to propose that Kean, as a moral leper, should be permanently banished from the stage — and the public's view. But the *Times*, unlike the *Theatrical Observer*, was not yet ready to call a halt. It noted, in its issue of 28th January that Kean, 'the obscene little personage', was to make another appearance at Drury Lane that evening. 'His real friends,' the *Times* went on, 'must now desert him, when they see him dead even to the lowest degree of shame which distinguishes human from animal nature.'

This time Edmund played Othello; and though the 'task of chastisement' was less noisily conducted than previously, it was just as ugly and persistent. He was continually subjected to lewd interruptions. Lines from his part that could be interpreted as references to his own private conduct were greedily pounced upon and hurled back at him. But the house was not as full as it had been before, and there were fewer mere demonstrators present as opposed to genuine patrons of the drama — people who, though they may have come as enemies to rend him for his moral turpitude, were paradoxically, what the

Times called his 'real friends'. They demanded a speech of apology from him at the end of his performance, and after some persuasion from Elliston he re-entered the stage in his day-clothes. They expected him to humble himself, but instead he called their bluff. 'If this is the work of a hostile Press', he said, 'I shall endeavour with firmness to withstand it; but if it proceeds from your verdict and decision, I will at once bow to it, and shall retire . . .'

Suddenly his supporters with cries of 'No! No!' and 'Kean forever!' appeared to have the only voice, because, much though they may have wished to humble the man, they could not bear the thought of losing the actor. The issue was really settled by that speech. In spite of the frantic efforts of his enemies Edmund had neither retreated nor begged for mercy. The odds had appeared to be overwhelming against him, but heroically he had refused to yield. The *Times* made several further attempts 'in the more distinguished part of the journal' to whip up mass hysteria. But it had played itself out. Though there were minor disturbances when Edmund acted Overreach on 31st January, these were so tame in comparison with what had gone before that it was evident that he would soon be allowed to perform in peace. By a supreme effort of will and courage he had restored order to his kingdom.

But he had not brought back peace to his own mind. He had been dealt cruel and shattering blows from which he would never recover.

For all his bragadoccio, he was an artist with an artist's sensitivity. And he had been paraded as a kind of monstrous freak for the delight of the masses. The true connoisseurs of the drama realized well enough that however base his personal habits might be, his histrionic powers were still matchless. But at the same time, now that his reputation had been so sensationally publicised, they could not forgive or forget it. They applauded the actor; but they would not shake hands with the man.

Socially he was ruined. Had he been in reality the complete vulgarian that he liked to paint himself, he would have accepted this fact with indifference. But he was a man who cried out pathetically for the admiration and respect of his fellows.

Unconsciously the *Times* prophesied correctly that he would not find adequate consolation 'among his wolves and his whores'. It was his misfortune that he had never found there a sufficient substitute for what he truly wanted. He had always longed, despite his fierce protestations to the contrary, to be a gentleman among gentlemen. Now he had placed himself forever beyond reach of gentility. And he found the realization unbearable.

He was bitterly unrepentant. Night after night at Drury Lane, although he was no longer being actively attacked, he lashed out at his unseen enemies in absurd, unrestrained, futile speeches. He made himself appear completely ridiculous. He was like a hurt bull charging madly about the arena where his tormentors lurked in safety. And like a bull, too, his suffering would seem endless.

At the beginning of April he departed on a tour of the provinces and the organized persecutions began all over again. In one town he was ostracized; in another he was hooted and pelted. In Manchester men walked through the streets with banners urging all decent playgoers to boycott the theatre where Edmund Kean was due to appear. Eventually a vast audience, consisting almost exclusively of males, succeeded in ruining his performance. The same thing happened in Glasgow. In Edinburgh, where the Presbyterian conscience was particularly alive, the manager of the playhouse was generally assailed for daring to engage the immoral actor upon whom no respectable woman could be expected to cast an eye. One public-spirited citizen stated, *coram populo*, that he would withdraw his patronage from the theatre if Kean were ever allowed to act in it again. This outburst drew a mild rebuke from the London periodical, *John Bull*:

> If Mr Kean were to be received at the gates of Edinburgh to be escorted by galloping cavalcades and made the associate of noble and virtuous women — we might say, 'For God's sake, Scotsmen, consider what you are doing — this man ... tipples and swears ... he is an adulterer, he is moreover a stage player — do not degrade your national

character by trashy processions for this wretched creature . . .'

But this is not asked of the Scotch people. Mr Kean is engaged to act, to do his professional business for their amusement.

That was the view already held in London, and it was miserable consolation to Edmund that he had, after the most galling experiences, saved his professional reputation from the total wreck of all his aspirations. No amount of applause from playgoers, separated from him by an insurmountable barrier, could make him forget the world's injustice or could alter the fact that his pride had been savagely mutilated.

Thomas Colley Grattan, his old friend, called on him some months after the trial, and was moved to pity by his mere appearance. 'I never saw a man so changed,' wrote Grattan who had last seen him in 1816, 'he had all the air of desperation about him. He looked bloated with rage and brandy; his nose was red, his cheeks blotched, his eyes bloodshot.' He dulled his pain not only with drink, but with the flattery that prostitutes could give him. Winston tells of an occasion when he arrived at the theatre about six in the morning, with two women and was with them until one o'clock when Dunn sent word that the women must leave. Afterwards, according to Winston, Edmund was very abusive and told Dunn that he gloried in being the blackguard that the town called him.

Again, Winston records in his diary for 16th March, 1825:

Kean, about three o'clock in the morning, ordered a hackney coach to his door, took a lighted candle, got in, and rode off. He was not heard of till the Thursday noon when they found him in his room at the theatre fast asleep wrapt up in a large white greatcoat. He then sent for a potence, some ginger, etc., and said, 'Send me Lewis* or the other woman. I must have a fuck, and then I shall do.' He had it. They let him sleep till about six, when they awoke him, dressed him, and he acted but was not very sober. After the play [we] got him to supper at Sigel's† lodgings and got him to a bedroom

---

*   Drury Lane actress.
†   Sic.

and locked him up till the morning.

But Grattan, whom Edmund had always liked, was given a glimpse, such as Winston never was, of the other side of his nature:

> The day I saw him, he sat down at the piano, nothwith-
> standing his agitated state of mind, and sang for me 'Lord
> Ullin's Daughter' with a depth and power and sweetness
> that quite electrified me. I had not heard him sing for many
> years; his improvement was almost incredible; his accompani-
> ment was also far superior to his former style of playing. I
> could not repress a deep sentiment of sorrow at the wreck he
> presented of genius, fame and wealth.

One would suppose from what Winston wrote of him in his diaries that Edmund entirely wasted his hours of leisure. One would be quite unaware that he was capable of great, if un-organized, generosity. As a certain Theodore Norton, one of his few apologists at the time of the trial, wrote in a poem called 'Kean':

> And low he was, and low did he descend,
> He stooped to prove himself the orphan's friend
> To take the helpless by the hand and give
> The starving wretch the future means to live;
> The dungeon he explored and burst the chain
> Of prisoned captives, — here was low again!
> His cloak upon a winter's piercing night
> (To shield a crippled beggar from its bite)
> He flung; and this, when rumoured in the west
> Was voted low again, as may be guessed.

Even when Edmund urged the merits of another actor whom he recommended for a job, Winston gives the impression that he was being tiresome rather than genuinely helpful. It was Edmund's real tragedy that he had a soul that belied his coarse behaviour. He suffered deep mortification of the kind that would have been impossible for the sort of man that Winston paints. Near the end of his life, he tried to express his tortured feeling in this cry of despair:

> What is this happiness of man?
> Its shadow, catch it if you can,
> Is it in Wealth and gay parade?
> Proud nature tells you, all must fade;
> She holds the key to human hearts
> Open to vice, and limpid darts,
> Carries her victim, in false pleasures' train,
> Raises to hope but soon to fall again.
> So drear, so desolate an abyss,
> You know not in the vortex that from this
> You feel the shock, but inward know no pain
> But drinking largely sets you right again.

9

On 21st July, 1825, Edmund wrote to Jack Hughes:

> Damn Drury and Buonaparte then for America ... I have promised a *Snuff Box* — *Brutus* to Major Downes, can send it down by my wife, who comes to Buxton on Sunday. I think you had better meet me in Edinburgh as I shall never be able to stand separations. I shall go to Greenock. I cannot return to London again. . . .

The meaning of the letter is unclear. One cannot be sure whether he had already decided on a separation from Mary. One does know, however, that Mary was utterly wretched, largely because her days of playing society hostess were obviously at an end. She blamed her misery entirely on Edmund, and though she had condoned his infidelity with Mrs Cox — she had, after all, been to Paris with him after the affair had become public knowledge — she could not forgive him his disgrace. She left him to endure his agony alone. Worse still, she added to his troubles by conducting a personal vendetta against him after the trial by assisting to drag his name through the mud.

She threatened to sell his property in Bute, lock, stock and barrel, and to collar the proceeds for herself. She put it about that he was suffering from venereal disease, and that she had caught it from him.

No doubt she was blinded by self-pity, and in her concern for her own future did not realize what she was about. Undoubtedly, after she had discovered that her husband was still capable of earning a very good living, she protested that she did not wish for a permanent separation from him. But whenever it was that the final rift took place, and however it was occasioned, her repentance came too late. Edmund's matrimonial affairs by the time he left for America in September were in the hands of lawyers.

Several letters passed between Henry Sigell, Edmund's solicitor, and Mary during the months of October and November. Mary's style varied from supplication to anger. On 6th October she wrote from Bute:

Tell me at once does he want me to remain here — will it give ease to his mind my doing so? Does he wish to see me again? Oh, pray answer these questions. I am too ill to leave here. I write from bed, and if I was well I cannot go without money ... I do not want a separation from my husband — not for worlds would I bring such a thing before the public — I thought it best to live away from him as he has behaved so strange — speak to me friendly and tell me Mr Kean's wishes — *all I can do I will*. ... Tell me truly what will make him happy? I am heart-broken.

In reply, Sigell explained that Edmund would make her an allowance of £504 per annum, out of which he would expect her to keep Charles at Eton and provide him with clothes. He would also let her have the use of the house at Bute, provided she made no attempt to sell the property. She would thus be able to live rent free. Sigell urged her to accept this offer:

It is in your power to restore to Mr Kean much of his lost happiness by acting up to his wishes ... If it is not too much to ask of you I should feel greatly indebted if you would spare me one of the many portraits you have of Mr Kean. I should like some token of remembrance of him in recollection of the many excellent qualities he possesses ... He left the USA in excellent health but almost heart-broken, his mind much depressed with conflicting thoughts.

This letter did not please Mary. The reference to Edmund's leaving 'in excellent health' alarmed her particularly, since she had made public the fact that he had venereal disease.

Sir Anthony Carlisle having attended me yesterday [she wrote], I told him I was made very uneasy by your saying that Mr Kean was quite free from ailment ... in that case my character must suffer, for if this can be proved what must be thought of me − Sir Anthony said '... Should the least hint be given that Mr Kean was not ill I shall come forward for your sake − leave it entirely to me − no one ever yet doubted the truth of my assertions' ... Mr Kean must pay Sir Anthony everything.

She was also furiously indignant, in spite of her previous pro-testations, that Edmund expected her to live in Bute. 'He has deprived me of health,' she wrote, 'the finest and greatest of blessings − happiness he has forever destroyed − my name he has taken from me and left me without any inquiry as to what I might need in the situation, the *dreadful* situation he left me.'

She herself had determined to leave Bute. She was not going to be kept there against her will. But she was peevishly angry at being baulked in her design to sell the property. 'No one will take charge of it,' she concluded exultantly. 'Take my word, Mr Kean will never live here, say what he likes. It is a sin to let it go to desolation, decay, and so see to it *directly*.'

By April 1826 Mary had taken rooms in London at No 6 Spring Street, Portman Square. She lived there with her son on an allowance which Edmund paid with faultless regularity, and which, though comparatively small, was sufficient to defray Charles's school fees at Eton and to satisfy her own immediate needs. She told Barry Cornwall, years later, that Edmund had 'parted very kindly with her' before his departure for America. That contradicts her first letter to Sigell, and is almost certainly untrue. Even if it is true, there is no doubt that he could not live with his family any longer. As the cast-off wife of a vicious man she was greatly pitied in her time and was deluged with sentiment by posterity. But in view of the facts, it may be wondered whether she was not, in a measure at least, responsible for her own misfortune.

10

Edmund looked on America as a place where he might be able to rebuild his fortune, which had been reduced to no more than a few hundred pounds, and restore his self-respect. In one of his more bombastic speeches at Drury Lane he had expressed the hope that 'for the honour of his countrymen, the machinations of his enemies would never be reported in Foreign Journals'. No doubt he had convinced himself as his ship approached New York, that American playgoers would be blissfully unaware of his mortal turpitude, and would rush to give him a wonderful reception. He was quite certain they must have forgotten all about that insult to their national pride he'd been accused of committing in Boston.

Of course, he harboured a sad illusion. The American public had been well fed by their Press with all the salacious details of the *Cox v. Kean* trial; and they were anyway thirsting for vengeance on this man who had insulted them. They were ready for him when he arrived.

He opened as Richard III in New York on 14th November. A huge audience filled the theatre, but he might just as well have stayed at home. Not a word he spoke could be heard above the noise of hisses and counter-hisses which was kept

up without a pause throughout the action of the play. Evidently, the Americans were determined to prove that they were
every bit as adept at staging Kean riots as the English.

In their detailed reports next morning, the newspapers said
that there had been more applause than anger, and that Kean's
enemies had been outnumbered by Kean's admirers. Just the
same, one may imagine what a terrible blow the very fact of the
disturbance had been to Edmund. He had come to America
for peace and he had found war. The persecution, from which
he had hoped to escape, was back with him again. He could
no longer bear it.

In desperation he fell back on his last line of defence. All
his life he had refused to beg for mercy, but now that he had
lost, not the nerve, but the spirit to go on fighting what else
could he do? The New York *Commercial Advertiser* had written:

> We think that no manager should allow such a lump of moral
> pollution to contaminate the boards. Every female must
> stay away and males hiss with indignation.

The New York *Daily Advertiser* had written: 'Americans, do
your duty just like London and Edinburgh.'

To these attacks and others of a similar kind, Edmund sent
the following reply, which was published in the *National
Advocate*:

> I visit this country now under different auspices and feelings
> than on a former occasion. Then I was an ambitious man,
> and the proud representative of Shakespeare's heroes: the
> spark of ambition is extinct, and I merely ask a shelter in
> which to close my professional and mortal career. I will
> give the weapon into the hands of my enemies; if they are
> brave they will not turn it against the defenceless.

This letter, though not as apologetic as it might have been,
stemmed the tide of public resentment against him. Its effect
proved that Edmund would certainly have minimised — might
even have avoided — his previous disasters had he chosen to

face them less aggressively. He conducted the remainder of his New York season not only peacefully but almost triumphantly. Before it ended he was able to send a £500 bill to Messrs Coutts, his London bankers. He was encouraged to regard his audiences as his friends again; and he could justly suppose that he was in truth beginning to rebuild his fortune.

But that first outburst of popular frenzy had shocked him none the less. He was now miserably apprehensive of the future, for he dared not foretell what would be the nature of his reception in other towns that he was contracted to visit. After all, he had learned from bitter experience to expect new troubles wherever he performed. Birmingham and Glasgow booed him months after he had restored order to Drury Lane. On this hypothesis peace in New York did not necessarily mean peace throughout America. On the contrary.

In his tortured state of mind he might have been tempted to turn tail and run. But even now he was no coward. Though he had been driven to a kind of self-abasement, he had lost none of his amazing courage. Otherwise, he would at least have cut out Boston — the town where, even in happier times, he had narrowly escaped being lynched.

He went there towards the end of December. He must have been fully aware of the fearful risk he was running, for on arrival he once again took up the shield of humility. From the Exchange Coffee House, where he was staying, he addressed a moving plea to the *Columbian Sentinel*, in which he besought the citizens of Boston to show him 'liberality and forbearance' instead of 'prejudice and cruelty'. 'That I have erred,' he wrote, 'I acknowledge . . . Acting from an impulse of irritation, I was certainly disrespectful to the Boston public; calm deliberation convinces me I was wrong. . .'

But this time his appeal for mercy was useless. Physical fear was an emotion that Edmund had never experienced. But he was forced to understand it on the night of 21st December, 1825, when he played Richard III in Boston.

All day long rumours of approaching vengeance had spread round the town. In the afternoon small boys had collected to jeer at the very placards on which Edmund's name was announced. In the early evening the street outside the theatre was already blocked by an angry, jostling crowd who had been unable to secure tickets of admission.

Edmund must have guessed what was in store for him as he walked through the stage door. He must have been certain of it as he sat in his dressing room putting on his make-up. For by then he knew that, although there was a packed house in front, not a woman was present. The audience was a sea of leering male faces.

Edmund stood in the wings listening to the uproar which had already begun. When the appalling moment came for him to make his entrance, he must have felt like a doomed prisoner mounting the guillotine. No wonder he looked pale and dejected.

But his enemies were pitiless. 'Off! Off!' they yelled, and pelted him with 'nuts, pieces of cake, a bottle of offensive drugs', anything they could find. Of course, he withdrew, but he was still ready to risk another onslaught. He sent a message through Mr Kilner, who was dressed up for the part of King Henry. 'Mr Kean wishes to make an apology,' Kilner announced, 'a humble apology from his heart and soul; but he will not do it at the risk of his life.'

This inspired the stockholders of the theatre who for obvious reasons wanted peace, to shout from the boxes 'Silence! Hear Kean! Let him apologize!' and so on. Edmund was sufficiently encouraged to venture on a second entry. But he came like a lamb to the slaughter. Once again he was greeted by howls of 'Off! Off!'; once again he was pelted without mercy; once again he was driven ignominiously from the stage. This time he rushed to the Green Room, where he flopped down and 'wept like a child'.

He wept tears of anguish and defeat. After having fought (and won) so many bitter duels with the public he was at last beaten and had to give in. A few minutes later a placard was brought on to the stage with the inscription, 'Mr Kean declines playing.' It was received with a bellow of unkind exultant laughter.

Meanwhile the situation looked ugly. Outside, the crowd had grown bigger, angrier, more restless. Inside, the rowdies

Sketch of Kean by T. Wageman.

(Top) 'The trip to Croydon' – a Cox v. Kean caricature, and *(bottom)* a caricature of Kean's first appearance at Drury Lane after the *Cox v. Kean* case.

were already beyond control. The management, afraid for Edmund's personal safety, smuggled him from the theatre by way of a back alley, 'through Mrs Powell's house'.

The audience were not content with driving Edmund off the stage. They wanted him back again – presumably so that they could drive him off once more. So they began shouting for him, and when they were informed that he had left the theatre, their fury knew no bounds. In the pit they rose up like a tidal wave, breaking up seats and smashing lamps and wrecking any other obstacles in their way. Presumably they intended to drag forth the luckless Kean from his hiding place and tear him limb from limb. Simultaneously, the crowd outside stormed the playhouse doors, the more respectable men in the boxes swung themselves up on to the windows twenty-five feet from the ground in an effort to get away and the confusion became so great that a semi-organized lynching expedition got caught up in a general riot. As a result only the theatre was damaged – and the public peace.

Edmund escaped. It was said that Tom Divol, a local hack driver, drove him to Brighton, where he took the stage coach to Worcester. He had seen the last of Boston. He had heard the last Bostonian shout. He must have sunk back in his seat wearily, dejectedly, but a little thankfully.

Before the end of the year he was back in New York, planning another successful season. On 31st December, he sent Mr W. Clarke, of Messrs Coutts, another bill for £500. 'I am convinced, Sir, from your great attention & politeness to me in England,' he wrote, 'that you will be pleased to hear that the wheels of fortune have once more turned in favour of an unjustly persecuted man.'

They hadn't – not entirely. During the next few months he played in Philadelphia, Charleston and Baltimore. In Philadelphia he was hissed on his first appearance, and in Baltimore another riot broke out. But nothing could disturb his will to go on. And inevitably, public opinion began to take his side. It realized that he had been punished to excess. 'Has any man been so persecuted as Mr Kean?' one newspaper asked. His sin was not particularly uncommon, particularly among actors.

Why, therefore, had he been singled out for such extraordinarily brutal treatment?

Most people recognized that he was still a supreme artist, and it seemed absurd after a while to deprive themselves of the pleasure of seeing and hearing him. Though his health had so badly deteriorated that to go through one of his famous characters completely exhausted him, yet he was still capable at his best of hiding his own weakness and mesmerising his audience. Sometimes he was forced to rest for weeks on end. But playgoers in general agreed with Dr Francis, who had remained his loyal friend, that his acting was (as Kemble once said of it) as much in earnest as ever. 'His Sir Giles in New York abated not of the vehemence and terror that characterized it as I had witnessed it at Old Drury in 1816,' the doctor wrote.

By the beginning of April Edmund had saved £2,250. He wrote to Cooper, stage manager at Drury Lane, telling him this joyful news, introducing a certain Mr Miller who was apparently seeking a London engagement, and also refuting Mary's later statement that he had parted from her 'very kindly'.

[Miller] is good enough to undertake the whole management of the *boat* which I shall call the United States, a trifling but sincere tribute of grateful feeling to a country that has given new life to my talent, my health & fortune ... I am not really the people's actor — but their Idol ... do you know anything of the unworthy being that bears my name? I hear she has left my paradise to spend that money in London which if she had an atom of maternal feeling should be hoarded for her son ...

That, of course, was not the letter of a truly happy man, but of a man deeply confused. He talked a great deal about death both in his speeches and in his conversation. Once, when he was with Dr Francis he threatened to throw himself from the roof of Bethlehem Asylum. Dr Francis seized hold of him and dragged him to safety. Otherwise he would have shared the fate of his father before him.

His friends feared for his reason. On one occasion he sud-

denly started to turn somersaults in a public park. On another
occasion he rushed out of his hotel in the middle of the night
wearing only his shirt, and awoke the whole street crying,
for no reason, 'Fire! Fire!'

Possibly these symptoms of mental unbalance were not so
much real as assumed to attract attention to himself and the
wrongs he had suffered. In moments of desperation he made
wild statements which he did not really mean. He said that
America was now his home and that he never wanted to see
England again. Yet he sent his savings back to London. He
scrutinized the English newspapers, too, and begged his cor-
respondents to tell him 'all about the affairs at Drury Lane'.

In his heart, he yearned to prove that he was still 'the first
English actor', and that he was capable of further triumphs.
He could never forget that he belonged to Drury Lane and
that Drury Lane by right belonged to him. But before he
could even contemplate a journey homewards he needed some
proof that he had vindicated himself, some indication that the
English people really wanted him back and would accept him,
not as their fallen player, but as their 'idol'.

During the summer of 1826, he visited Canada. And there,
possibly because he was so obviously owed reparation, Fortune
suddenly shined on him in all her radiance. He acted in Montreal and Quebec, and in both towns he was given a wonderful,
exhilarating reception of a kind which he really appreciated
and which he had not known for long enough. Audiences
flocked to see his performances and applauded him with royal
acclamations. Still more important, he was flattered and lionized
and entertained by the leaders of society. He was treated like
an ambassador of the theatre. In Montreal he was entertained
at a public dinner. During his speech he said: 'How shall I
thank those beings who have kindled the social spark, almost
extinct, and have lighted up my heart again to friendship and
esteem? . . . It will enliven those who in spite of my inconsis-
tencies and errors, watch with anxious eyes my progress, and
whose grateful hearts will beat like mine at the receipt of
friendship which restores me to the rank of gentleman!'

He was made a gentleman in Montreal, and in Quebec he was

made a King. He was received into the Huron tribe of Red Indians. The ceremony was elaborately conducted in the presence of four native tribesmen and several other local celebrities, including Captain Sir William Wiseman of HMS *Jupiter*. He was given the exalted rank of Alanienouidet.

The disgraced actor, the pernicious adulterer, the social outcast had become Alanienouidet, the Red Indian Chief. Edmund felt sure that it would silence his most obstinate 'enemies' and make even the *Times* bow to him. For was he not, in truth, a kind of King?

Momentarily, this meant more to him than all his Drury Lane triumphs put together. Over and over again he played, in his own imagining, the part of Alanienouidet and his wonderful exploits — his feats of horsemanship, his stirring speeches, his wise and powerful rule. To add the zest of realism to his daydreams, he painted his face and decked himself out in his tribal costume whenever he could find the faintest excuse to do so — either in public or in private. He had special visiting cards printed with Edmund Kean on one side and Alanienouidet on the other.

After Edmund's return to New York, Dr Francis received a mysterious command to call on a certain Red Indian Chief at his hotel. Dr Francis obeyed, and was shown into a long, darkened room, lighted up by many rays from floor lamps . . . surrounding a stage or throne. Seated in great state was the chief. 'A more terrific warrior I never saw . . . His eye was meteoric and fearful, like the furnace of the cyclops. He vociferously exclaimed, "Altatenaida!".' And it was only then that Dr Francis recognized his friend, Edmund Kean.

Edmund had decided to go back to London. His Canadian experience had heartened him enormously. Besides, he had always said, even in his blackest moments, that his one remaining ambition was to control the destinies of Drury Lane.

Now his chance seemed to have come at last. Elliston had failed to pay the rent of the theatre, and had been forced by the proprietors to resign. Someone of influence had written to Edmund that the vacant lesseeship would be his for the asking.

He was very ill when he sailed from America on 8th December. But his spirits were buoyed up by more than brandy. He was confident of a gala reception in his own country. He had triumphed over his enemies. Now he was returning home as Alanienouidet, the Red Indian Chief, soon to be crowned at last the rightful King of Drury Lane.

PART THREE

The End and the Beginning

1

Edmund was never to be crowned King of Drury Lane. Either he'd been made the victim of a cruel hoax or he'd been double-crossed by Stephen Price, the new lessee, who himself came from New York. It was no wonder that Winston, who stayed on as House Manager under Price until the middle of 1827, should record in his diary of 4th January that Kean arrived at the theatre 'very drunk ... about four in the afternoon, put himself in a very great rage because Liston's things were in his room. He shortly after went away in a great rage.'

Yet by 8th January even Winston had to admit that Kean acted 'remarkably well'. He had signed with Stephen Price to appear an agreed number of nights at the colossal salary of one hundred guineas a performance. He had chosen to open as Shylock, not for reasons of sentiment, but because during the lengthy intervals between the big scenes he would have time to rest and husband his strength for another supreme effort.

Dr Doran, the stage historian, still treasured in his old age the memory of the shout that greeted Kean on his entrance. He had never before, and had never since, heard one so loud. To him it signified the complete reconciliation between the actor and his public.

And so, in a sense, it did. But the fashionable people who sat in front and cheered and clapped their hands were not seen in the Green Room afterwards. To them Kean would always be socially taboo. He had committed an intolerable offence not so much against morals as against caste.

Edmund himself lay uncomfortably in bed at Hummum's Hotel in Covent Garden, playing with the trappings of Alanie-nouidet, drinking brandy and water and looking dejectedly into the future. True, he had climbed back on to his histrionic pedestal. But something he was sure he valued more than a myriad successes on the stage — his honour and prestige as a man — still eluded him.

I have said that Winston's diaries, now that I have read them, have not materially changed my view of Edmund Kean; moreover that some of the entries are mere repetitions of gossip. For instance, Winston records that on 4th February, 1827, he has been told by Price that Kean 'allows Mrs Kean £600 a year for herself and son. She has twice annoyed him with visits while in England, and he therefore removed to the Fountain.' That information would be of considerable interest, if one could rely on its accuracy. But can one? It must have been a while immediately before or after this that Grattan called on Kean, not at Fountain Court in the Strand, which was where the Wolves Club used to meet, but at the Hummum's Hotel. Grattan had written a play, called *Ben Nazir*, especially for Kean, but after the Cox trial he had abandoned hope that it would ever be produced. He was convinced then that Kean's career was ruined, but now that the fallen man seemed to have staged a histrionic come-back, his hopes for *Ben Nazir* were revived.

Of course, he did not minimize Edmund's moral and physical abasement. He had only to look at him to realize how grossly he had deteriorated even in the last year. 'He presented,' Grattan wrote, 'a mixture of subdued fierceness, unsatisfied triumph and suppressed dissipation.'

When Grattan called on Edmund he was ushered into his hotel bedroom by a black boy in livery. He found Edmund propped up in bed, holding court as the Huron Chieftain. With one hand he grasped a tomahawk; with the other he was aimlessly engaged in making up his face 'for a savage look'. A supply of hot white wine was placed within his reach.

By the window, at the far end of the untidy room, an unknown artist, his form partially hidden behind the easel, was painting Alanienouidet's portrait. Two grubby courtiers lounged near Edmund's bed; they were apparently assisting their master to while away the hours by drinking copiously of his liquor.

When Grattan walked in Edmund rolled his eyes, flourished his tomahawk, and then, as if satisfied that these theatrical tactics had produced their effect, shook him warmly and sensibly by the hand. He must have warned his hired artist and his attendant satellites that Grattan, a dramatist who had written a tragedy for him, was coming, for they soon excused themselves; having drained their tumblers and spouted some extravagant farewell compliments, they took their leave. Edmund and Grattan were left in peace to discuss *Ben Nazir*.

But a little while later their interview was interrupted by the unheralded entrance of two veiled young ladies, who flitted mysteriously through the room. Edmund explained, *sotto voce*, that they were the daughters of a respectable clergyman, and were both madly in love with him. Grattan, however, from the brief glimpse he had of them formed a less flattering opinion of their station in society.

Inevitably Grattan decided that Edmund had 'lost all the respectability of private life'. He realized, too, that he was suffering from a painful malady. Among other things he had an ulcerated leg which was so bad he was in danger of having it amputated. Yet Grattan was satisfied that his acting was as great as it had ever been. The critics, in their most recent accounts, had all said so.

As an artist Edmund himself still inspired trust. He assured Grattan, with the most disarming confidence, that *Ben Nazir* would be a *succes fou*. He predicted it would run for a hundred nights. He had decided to spend fifty guineas on a costume of special magnificence — over and above any dress allowance the Drury Lane management might make him. He had made arrangements for his portrait to be engraved in character. He had ordered his next annual wherry to be called *Ben Nazir*. And apart from these flourishes of enthusiasm, he seemed genuinely determined to work hard at his part. He kept a prompt copy of the play under his pillow. He had already begun to study his lines.

At the end of February Edmund left London to fulfil a series of provincial engagements. According to Winston, he had sent John Lee, the man who had acted as his secretary in America and had returned with him, to look after his estate in Bute. Edmund played in Manchester, Dublin and Edinburgh, and in each of these towns he received ovations just as thunderous as those which had welcomed him back to Drury Lane. However, in Dublin he appeared one night as Alanienouidet and harangued his audience with a long megalomaniacal speech. This was reported in the Press as another of Kean's futile efforts to impress people with his importance. Grattan was slightly alarmed when he read of it. It augured ill, he thought, for *Ben Nazir*.

But at the beginning of May Edmund returned to London apparently invigorated and in a calm, conscientious state of mind. He set Grattan's fears at rest. He took lodgings at Duke Street, Adelphi, and embarked eagerly on a new routine of life, which was quiet and sheltered. He renounced alcohol, went to bed every night before eleven o'clock and shunned low company.

Ben Nazir was put into rehearsal at Drury Lane. It was to be produced on 21st May. Edmund had been present at the first two rehearsals, when he delighted Grattan with the vigour and intelligence of his reading. He excused himself from attending the remaining rehearsals on the grounds that his fellow actors disturbed his concentration and that he preferred to work in the peace and solitude of his own surroundings.

Every morning after breakfast Edmund ordered his carriage and drove in it to Kensington Gardens, where he spent two hours in the shade of the trees, studying his part. In the afternoons he sometimes had himself rowed in his wherry on the Thames. He lay comfortably back, the book of *Ben Nazir* in his hands, and spouted away for the benefit of the watermen and the *naiades*. In the evenings Grattan generally kept him company at Duke Street. Grattan came as a kind of guardian angel. He wanted to make sure that Edmund was not tempted into the night by any of his unwanted guests. He never left him until he was safely in bed. When 21st May arrived at last there was no doubt in Grattan's mind that Edmund had worked hard and undistractedly, although he refused to attend even the final rehearsal.

None the less, there was cause for apprehension. In the

morning Grattan went alone to Edmund's lodgings to wish him
luck. He found him striding about the drawing-room, arrayed
in his gorgeous stage costume and declaiming his part with the
utmost conviction. He was conducting his own private dress
rehearsal. He seemed excited, proud and brimful of confidence.
And he boasted that *Ben Nazir* could not possibly fail.

This was all very reassuring. But Grattan noticed with dismay
that Edmund still carried a prompt copy of the play in his
hands. He spoke his lines magnificently, but not without the
aid of the written text.

Grattan did not give up hope. He was nervous when he took
his place at the theatre — well hidden from the public view in
a small private box near the side of the stage. He had resigned
himself to the fact that Kean would be 'fluffy' and uncertain;
but he felt confident that the actor's experience would pull
him through and that his imperfections, however numerous,
would not be glaringly apparent to the audience. Although he
feared a rough, unpolished performance, he did not anticipate
disaster. There would be time for improvement later. Allowances
had to be made for an opening performance in a new character.

But if Grattan had had the power to see through the curtain
at that moment, he would probably have refused to allow his
play to go on. All Edmund's self-confidence had fallen from
him like a loosely girt mantle. He was in his dressing room
weeping his heart out — so nervous and so miserable that he
had not the spirit to change into his costume. The curse which
strikes most actors in their old age had hit him cruelly in the
prime of life. He was a player who could no longer learn a part.
In spite of all his efforts, all his good resolutions, he had failed
to make the lines of *Ben Nazir* lodge in his memory.

Day after day, up to the last moment, he had avoided the
truth and had tried to delude himself into thinking 'that everything would be all right on the night'. But now when his memory
was still barren of all but a very few of the words he should
speak, he realized that such miracles do not happen. If he had
been unable to say his lines in the quiet and solitude of his own
surroundings, how much less able would he be to repeat them
in full view of a critical audience. Inevitably he would disgrace

himself and ruin the first play of a man who was his friend.

Wallack, the stage manager, suggested he should ask for a postponement, and, according to Winston, Edmund kept the play waiting for half an hour. But eventually he dried his eyes, put on his make-up and walked down to the stage in a kind of stupor.

He looked extraordinarily impressive in his rich costume of which he had been so proud. The audience cheered him wildly and settled down to enjoy what they supposed would be a fine performance. But Grattan was appalled. He curled up in his seat. He knew now that his worst fears were going to be fulfilled.

> The intention of the author and the keeping of the character [wrote Grattan] required him to rush rapidly upon the stage, giving utterance to a burst of joyous soliloquy. What was my astonishment to see him, as the scene opened, standing in the centre of the stage, his arms crossed and his whole attitude one of thoughtful solemnity! ... He spoke, but what a speech! The one I wrote consisted of eight or nine lines: *his* was of two or three sentences, but not six consecutive words of the text. His look, his manner, his tone, were to *me* quite appalling; to any other observer they must have been incomprehensible. He stood fixed, drawled out his incoherent words and gave the notion of a man who had been half-hanged and then dragged through a horsepond. . .

As it had begun, so it went on. There was no reprieve. A cold sweat broke out on Grattan's brow, and he experienced a feeling of revulsion of which he was ashamed. But he remained in his secluded seat to endure the cumulative agony of a fiasco. He watched his play being mutilated, and his reputation as a dramatist being sacrificed on the altar of Kean's 'exhaustion and decay'.

When the curtain fell on the first act, there was complete silence — 'the voiceless verdict of damnation'. According to Winston, Kean was repeatedly hissed during the play, and at

the end there was loud booing. James Wallack came to offer
Kean's apologies. The audience shouted at him abusively
until he announced that *Ben Nazir* was withdrawn, and that
in its place next Thursday Mr Kean would appear as Sir Giles
Overreach. Then, illogically enough, they cheered him lustily.

Grattan braced himself to go behind the scenes. He thanked
his actors, who, in their turn, commiserated with him. He saw
Edmund being led off the stage by two dressers, and spoke to
him as consolingly as possible. But Edmund was too upset to
say much in reply. He merely bowed his head, waved his hand
despairingly and muttered some half-choked, incoherent words
of regret.

Next morning the newspaper critics — with few exceptions —
were more derogatory of the play than of the acting. The *Times*,
for example, while admitting — *en passant* — that Kean was
imperfect, reserved its main invective for Grattan. No player,
it concluded, could have saved the tragedy of *Ben Nazir* from
the fate which it had encountered and had deserved. No doubt
that was true. But if *Ben Nazir* had been the finest tragedy ever
written, it could not have survived Kean's performance.

This would never have been understood either by his contemporaries or, very likely, by posterity, if Edmund had attempted to shelter behind the Press notices. He had already admitted,
through Wallack, that he had been responsible for the failure of
Ben Nazir, and he never tried afterwards to shift the blame on
to Grattan, who was his friend. In his own mind there was no
escape from the truth. 'He had ruined a fine play', he said, and
in so doing had disgraced himself.

A few days later Grattan returned to France, disillusioned
and determined he would have no more concern with the
theatre. But before he left he went to bid Edmund farewell. He
had every reason, of course, to be angry with him, and yet when
he saw him, broken and miserable and tragically repentant, he
could feel for him nothing but sorrow. He forgot his own
grievance in his compassion for the man who had caused it. It
was, after all, impossible for Grattan to recriminate against
someone who was obviously helpless and infinitely more injured
than he was himself. Grattan had met with a temporary set-back.

He was disappointed. But he was still a young man, and before him stretched a life rich and varied.

Edmund, on the other hand, had suffered a crowning blow. Already he had lost home, health, honour, position — the things which, in retrospect, he valued as a man. Now he had been forced to realize that even as an actor he was crippled. Winston's diary of 9th May reads: 'Kean told me last night that he meant after the present season to build a schooner and go to sea, having six men to work the vessel which would cost £15,000 etc, etc, go to America, the West Indies, Botany Bay, etc.' If Edmund meant what he said — and one may doubt it — he was dreaming an impossible dream. For the next six years he would continue working, fighting, earning, spending, lusting, hating, drinking, regretting, indulging in false pleasures that gave him no joy, and seeking the peace that consistently eluded him. He, too, was still a young man; he was thirty-nine. But there was nothing before him save death. He would slither towards it painfully, slowly and unwillingly. But he would go towards it directly.

2

Edmund was like the captain of a damaged vessel who, in spite of the inevitable end, continually puts out to sea. His estate on the Island of Bute, which he still owned and still cherished, thus proving once again how little Mary understood him, was his harbour. He would never afford to stay there long. But he always welcomed the chance of going there, and he pined for his 'paradise' while he was away from it. He wrote to Dan M'Corkindale in the summer of 1827:

> ...You will oblige me by acting as my agent during the interval of absence & direct Reid to let me find the grounds on my return as I have been accustomed to see them. I do not understand gardening techniques, but they have always looked very beautiful and beautiful I wish them to remain.

My health is very fast improving & the public favour greatly
increasing, and yet I do not know how it is, amidst the blaze
of popularity that is naturally attendant upon the favourites
of caprice, I cannot help envying the poorest peasant that
doffs his cap to the visitor of Rothesay — however, if the
world & my profession prevent my living there, it remains
with myself the power of dying there, & even that I look
forward to with gratification. . . .

At Bute Edmund sought happiness in a world of make-believe
which he had fashioned from the paradoxes of his nature. He
glorified the past and planned for the future and pretended that
the present was not fleeting. He revealed all his conflicting
faults and virtues — his generosity and his jealousies, his simplicity and his love of display, his craving for solitude and his
plungings into dissipation.

Since his return from America, he had lavished a small
fortune on improving his property. He had had a road built
through the woods, so that he could now drive from Rothesay
to his front gates in his own coach. The local workmen had
warned him beforehand that the road would cost him a great
deal of money. But he had replied confidently that he would
earn enough to pay for it from a three nights' engagement at
Glasgow. Above the gates he had placed four busts — one of
Shakespeare, one of Massinger, one of Garrick and one of himself. When the moon showed up their whiteness after dark they
looked like spectres and frightened the peasants. On the night
that they had been unveiled Edmund had given a firework
display and had invited half the inhabitants of Rothesay to
attend it.

He had papered the walls of his drawing-room with an
expensive wall-paper which had been specially designed for him
in Paris and which depicted scenes from his famous plays. In
his wardrobe he kept a supply of stage costumes. Sometimes he
would wander about his grounds dressed up as Richard or Overreach. More often he would appear in a kilt or in a loud tartan
suit.

He pictured himself, through a fog of tinsel, as a great lord living in retirement. He had a moss house built for him on a mound which was sheltered by the trees. He used to sit in it for hours on end and gaze down on Sweet Loch Fad and on the country beyond. Above the entrance to his moss house these words were inscribed:

T'is Glorious
Through the loopholes
of
Retreat
To Peep at such a world.

And beneath the inscription was placed his 'coat of arms'!

When he spent his birthday at Woodend (as he did in March, 1829) he would order a blunderbuss to be fired in the morning as a kind of royal salute. In the evening he would give a dinner party to his notable acquaintances from Rothesay.

He entertained on a lavish scale. But he was a surprising host. Before the meal ended he would invariably find some pretext to rush from the room, having changed into fancy dress. Then he would embark on a song or a recitation and would expect his guests to applaud him effusively.

But in spite of these curious displays, so alien to his surroundings, he was by no means unpopular with the natives of the island. He was in the first place free and easy with his money, and a wonderful patron of local labour and local trade. John Duncan the draper, Nanny Lochley the butcher, and the Old Mill Shop, where he bought his groceries, were all very thankful for his custom. And with his extensive building operations he put a deal of work in the way of Robert Orkney the mason and Archibald Mackirdy the joiner and John Crawford the handyman. He paid handsomely for it, too. There was nothing mean about him.

His servants on the estate — born and bred in Bute — were devoted to him. And though they were convinced he was fabulously rich, he did not have to buy their respect. They had an instinctive understanding of his true qualities. They were mystified, of course, by his eccentricities. But they were drawn to him because of his generosity and modesty and simplicity and his gay love of their own country.

John Reid the gardener lived with his family in the lodge by the front gates. He had a daughter, who was a small child at the time, but who later became Mrs M'Fie and who was still alive at the beginning of the present century. She had the most charming recollections of Edmund.

I min' Kean liked a wee drap, and he always came into the lodge for it every time he passed out or in the gate. He had a press there to keep it in, but he would never take it unless my mother was there to give it to him. Any time we saw him coming along we would run and tell my mother, 'There's Mr Kean coming', and she always had it ready for him.

Edmund gave her a pony, so that she could ride in and out of Rothesay by herself. And once he gave her and her mother tickets for a performance of *Richard III* at Glasgow. Sometimes afterwards he asked her whether she had enjoyed it. As she had not recognized him in his make-up, she remarked naively that 'Richard was a very ugly man'. Edmund laughed delightedly at this. 'Ah,' said Mrs M'Fie, 'Kean was a very kind man and very charitable to all around him.'

He liked to be with children, perhaps because he had himself a child's inquisitiveness about animals and flowers and all the other things in Nature that he did not understand. He used to be seen carrying Bailie Muir's son on his back, or walking about his grounds with Sandy Nisbet, the herdboy, by his side (he called him the 'cow boy'). Sandy Nisbet, like Mrs M'Fie, lived to be an octogenerian, and he too had his tender memories of Edmund.

He was very fond of hearing me speak Gaelic [said Sandy]. He always carried a bottle containing wine or red stuff, and plenty of bread and cheese. One day, when taking lunch outside, there were some sheep feeding about, a black sheep among the flock. 'Do you know, Sandy,' he asked me, 'why black sheep do not eat as much grass as white ones?' 'Well,

I don't know, sir,' I replied, 'unless it is because there are not so many black sheep as white ones.'

For this information Edmund gave Sandy half a sovereign. And he gave him a whole sovereign when he learned that his mother could speak nothing but Gaelic!

Sandy also said of Edmund:

He was always very fond of sitting at a big oak near a burn that comes down from the Glen at Woodend. He would be looking at some little trout in the burn, and one day he said to John Reid that if he died in Scotland he would like to be buried beside that tree.

Edmund dropped all his pretences when he was with children; he had a touching respect for their innocence, and expected others to respect it too. Once he caught his coachman, whose name was William Bedlam, amusing himself by shooting a bonnet off Sandy's head. He flew into a rage and snatched the pistol from Bedlam's hand. 'If it wasn't for your wife and family,' he shouted dramatically, 'you would never handle a rein for me again.' 'He was a drunken devil, that coachman,' said Sandy, 'but Kean would never say a word to him for that.'

Neither Sandy Nisbet nor Mrs M'Fie had much to tell of the life Edmund led inside his house. That was largely hidden from them. Sandy said that Edmund had little regard for the Sabbath, that he stayed in bed till the late afternoon and then went fishing on the loch. Mrs M'Fie remembered that after his return from America he used to come to Bute with a woman whom he called Mrs Kean but who was not his wife, 'An awfu' bonny woman'.

Her real name was Ophelia Benjamin, and she may have been identical with an unnamed woman described by Winston in his entry of 6th February, 1827. This reads in part:

Kean came to Massingham [D.L. doorkeeper] about eight this evening with a female with him. I happened to pass at the time, and he asked if he might take in the lady. I said, 'Certain-

ly.' He went in, and at nearly twelve he came with her into
my room, was uncommonly civil, said she had come all the
way from America to act and he wished her to play Amanthis
[in Inchbald's *Child of Nature*, 1788] but he would not play
the Marquis [of Almanza]. He was drunk; she kept her eye, a
sharp one, upon him and was silent.

Whether or not that was Ophelia, it is certain that he had
taken a mistress to live with him by the summer of 1827, for
about that time he wrote to his tailor: 'I forgot this morning
to tell you, my wife wants a plaid silk coat. Send it with mine
on Monday. *Oh these women are damned plagues.*'

Ophelia certainly had a 'sharp eye'. Her surname was Benjamin, and by nationality she was an Irish Jewess. According
to one account, she was the daughter of a tailor and a prostitute, the sister of a professional bruiser. She was undoubtedly
a hardened strumpet herself; she was young, strong, unscrupulous and frequently tipsy.

She had no affection and no respect for Edmund. She regarded him as a weak-willed, doddering, profligate old fool
who was crazy for her well-used body. She was abusively rude
to him. She humiliated him in public. When she could not get
her own way by any other means, she resorted to physical
violence. One celebrated instance of this was immortalized in
these lines:

> The lesser tribe of low buffons,
> And high flown tragic ranters,
> Had plenteous showers of knives and spoons,
> And volleys of decanters.
>
> I'll pull the house about the ears
> Of each belligerent Tyke,
> And like the sun let fall (she cry'd)
> My beams on all alike
>
> Full late the pair returned to sup;
> For after several rounds,

Inglorious Richard gave it up,
And gave her fifty pounds.

Ophelia added enormously to the isolation and degradation that
Edmund experienced during the last years of his life. She had
virtually cut him off from all but his tavern subjects, and she
delivered a crushing blow when he was in Bute in June of 1820.
His secretary, Phillips, protested to her about her wanton
disregard of economy in running the house. She answered his
complaint so insultingly that he decided he could not stay
another minute in Edmund's employ. From Rothesay he
wrote to Edmund explaining the circumstances of his hurried
departure and apparently announcing his resignation. This was
no less of a shock to Edmund because he now had a second
secretary, John Lee, whom, according to Winston, he had
brought back with him from America and had sent up to look
after his estate as soon as he got back. He wrote this reply to
Phillips who had been with him for at least ten years:

> Dear Phillips:
> I am shocked but not Surprised. in error I was born in error
> have I lived in error I shall die, that a *gentleman* should be
> insulted under my roof creates a blush that I shall carry to
> my grave, and that you are so in every sense of the word is
> unquestionable. from Education, Habit and manners. it is too
> true that I have fostered a worm till it has become a viper but
> my guilt is on my head, farewell . . .

Edmund despised Ophelia, yet he was her slave. He wanted to
be rid of her, yet in his decay could not do without her. He
was bound by the shackles of his own physical desires. And
he had resigned himself to his fate.*

Phillips had left, and Edmund was powerless to do the one
thing that would bring him back. Not long afterwards he wrote
these lines to the 'viper':

I break your slumber, sweet but pray forgive
For you alone my love I wish to live.

---

*   See appendix.

3

At the beginning of the 1827–1828 Drury Lane season, Edmund quarrelled with Stephen Price, and as a result he broke with the theatre where he had won his fame, and went over to Covent Garden, which was now managed by Charles Kemble, John Philip's brother. Despite his failing powers, and his proven inability to learn a new part, he was still a huge attraction, still the 'first English actor', and at Covent Garden the public crowded excitedly to see him.

On most nights he could summon enough energy to electrify his audience, and to make his famous characters seem vigorously alive. Only those behind the scenes knew for certain how much of his strength was artificial. Before his entrances he sat in a chair in the wings, his face blotched and puffy and distorted under its make-up, his body bent double with exhaustion. He sipped continually at a glass of brandy and hot water. He called impatiently to his dresser, who hovered near him, for another glass 'stronger and hotter'. Someone gave him his cue warning. 'He looked about, as from a dream, and sighed, and painfully got to his feet, swayed like a column in an earthquake,'* then gathered himself together, stood erect and walked firmly on to the stage.

But though he seldom disappointed those in front, his attacks of illness, which kept him off the stage, were now so frequent and so serious, that it seemed clear he was fighting a losing battle with death. Young men who would prattle about his splendour to their grandchildren, and old men who had thrilling memories of his first achievements wanted to see him again and yet again before it was too late. At the age of forty he was already history. And he had the glamour and pathos about him that invariably attaches to history which yet lives.

He himself encouraged the popular suspicion that his career was approaching its close. He often threatened retirement. In

---

*   *Their Majesties' Servants* by Dr. John Doran, Wm Allan 1865.

his speeches he let it be known that he would not bother the
world much longer with his presence. And yet, while he posed
as a figure of the past, he tried bravely to believe in his own
future. Time after time he collapsed, but recovered amazingly
and plunged once more into the fray.

He did not shrink from taking on any fresh engagement,
however arduous. In May of 1828, he went over to Paris to
act for Emile Laurent, who had established a company of
English players at the Odeon theatre. He opened a two months'
season on 12th May, and one may judge how busy he had been
before then by this letter, which he had written to Laurent in
January:

> I am sorry you did not apprise me of your wishes previous
> to your departure from London, as I should then have made
> any sacrifices on my part to have complied with them, it is
> now not in my power as I have made theatrical engagements
> in Yorkshire which will fill up my time until the seventh of
> May . . . A word once given cannot in honour be revoked . . .

The French playgoers did not give Edmund a very heartening
reception. In April they had been swept off their feet by
Macready, and now they found Kean unexciting by comparison.
Of course, they had been expecting too much of him. They
knew him only by his tremendous reputation, and made no
allowance for his weakness and fatigue. Though he had been
well heralded in their Press, they had never seen him before and
were not hypnotised by any lingering memories of his former
glories. Inevitably, they were disappointed in him, because
they judged him unsentimentally and strictly on his own
merits. They were dazzled by his occasional flashes, but on the
whole they decided that his light flickered feebly beside the
brilliant star of Macready.

Edmund returned to England at the end of June, moody and
disgruntled. He had hoped to win fresh laurels in Paris, and
instead he had been engulfed in the aftermath of another's
triumph. It was unwholesome medicine for a dying man.

Throughout the summer he went on fulfilling provincial

engagements. But he had decided that he was in need of a long rest. On 27th August he wrote from Liverpool to the Covent Garden manager:

> I wrote you from Southampton, requesting you to favour me with a line at Liverpool, this is more than a month since I stated that the longer leave of absence you allowed me the more I shou'd feel obliged. I play here till Monday next, & intended then to put my helm towards the Isle of Bute, if you and the Winds permit. I beg you therefore to let me have my orders instanta, & I shall implicitly obey command.

He spent September in Bute, and did not reappear at Covent Garden until 13th October. But by then his health was so far improved that he was able to carry on for nearly three months without a breakdown, which by this time was a considerable achievement for him. Not that he was by any means well. The quality of his performances varied from night to night, according to his physical condition. One may judge this from reading the criticism in any contemporary periodical. For example, one finds in the *Theatre* that his Richard on 13th October was 'very tame and unimpressive'. His pauses were often misplaced through breathlessness. However on 16th October his Shylock was so bold and vivid that criticism was disarmed and plunged into verse:

> What ere thine errors, Kean, what ere thy shame
> We cannot part with thee, we cannot cease,
> To own thy worth: enjoy thy well-earned fame,
> And may that fame still with the years increase!
> Thou art the Sun's bright child — then pause and let
> Prudence direct thee, for thy sun must set.

But even this mood of ecstasy was impermanent. On 30th October his Othello was pronounced to be 'sinking gradually into a premature debility both of body and mind'.

And yet he was doing his best to merit the public's applause and the gratitude of his new employers. From 17th November to 3rd December Covent Garden had to be closed down because of a gas explosion, and the company played during the interim at the English Opera House. In the circumstances of financial loss, which inevitably resulted from the move, Edmund declined to accept more than half his salary.

He gave an even better proof of his devotion to duty when he agreed to attempt a new character. He chose the name part in *Virginius*, a play, by his old friend Sheridan Knowles, which had originally been intended for him. In spite of his traumatic experience of a year ago, and in spite of his inner certainty that his memory was irreparably impaired, he embarked on the perilous task of learning lines which he had never spoken before and which had already been made famous by his foremost rival, Macready.

And by an extraordinary, superhuman exertion of his will, he succeeded. It cost him days of anguish, anxiety and despair, but in the end he knew his part. On 15th December, after repeated announcements and withdrawals on the bills, he appeared as Virginius.

He created little sensation in the character — far less than he had hoped for. Criticism, on the whole, ranked him far inferior to Macready.

His parting with the child was exquisitely played, and in the more subdued parts he was eminently successful. But when Virginius is made a slave, rage appeared more the frothy ebullitions of a choleric man than the terrible indignation of a noble Roman. His physical powers are unable to execute his design. In all scenes requiring great exertions he became exhausted. . . .

No doubt his performance had the sad blemishes of his own weakness. And yet it was an heroic effort, and deserved more generous recognition and wider sympathy than the handsome tortoiseshell snuff-box, lined with gold, which was presented to him after the final rehearsal 'as a trifling but cordial acknowledgement of his most valuable assistance and most liberal conduct. . . . by his brother performers'.

The strain of learning *Virginius* heralded another collapse. On 12th January Edmund was taken ill in his dressing-room immediately before a performance, and had to return to bed. A few weeks later he left London for the avowed purpose of enjoying a protracted convalescence at Bute.

Edmund extended a warm invitation to Charles Kemble to join him there, but Kemble politely declined. The reason was very probably the presence of Ophelia. It was certainly the reason why his son Charles refused to sleep in the house when he paid Edmund a visit at Bute.

Charles was now a young man of eighteen, and was on the stage. As an Eton schoolboy two years earlier, he had angered Edmund by declining a cadetship in the East India Company that his father had found for him. Hillebrand* accepts Cornwall's account of the reasons for Charles's behaviour on the grounds that Mary probably supplied Cornwall with the information. But, as I have said, Mary was a most unreliable historian, and in this case if she said that she was receiving an annuity of only £200 her word was directly contradicted in Sigell's offer to her, on Edmund's behalf, of an annuity of £504. That may later have been increased, for an entry in Winston's diary of 4th February, 1827, says that Kean was allowing Mrs Kean £600 a year for herself and her son. Possibly, it is safest to go no further in trying to account for Charles's refusal than to quote Winston's diary of 26th February, 1827, which reads:

At the end of *Richard III* this evening, Wallack made an apology for Kean, who was ill. He finished the part but seemed not with that force and energy he was accustomed to; and, when dead, instead of remaining till the curtain dropped, he was carried off the stage. It seems he was not only ill in body but in mind. Having procured for his son (between sixteen and seventeen) from Mr Calcraft a cadetship, his son, Charles, came from Eton this day and refused to accept — said he had a gentleman's education and could do

---

*   *Edmund Kean*, New York, Columbia University Press, 1933.

without his father's aid, etc.

It was no doubt with his mother's backing that Charles became an actor. He began at the top. Simultaneously with Edmund's breakaway to Covent Garden, he made his debut at Drury Lane as Young Norval in *Douglas*.

It was a stunt, of course, engineered by Stephen Price, and deservedly it failed. The boy Kean had no training, and very little natural talent. The critics handled him roughly and the public quickly lost interest in him. Charles soon realized despite his mother's blandishments that he was not yet ready to face a London audience. So he went into the provinces, though he never had to endure such hardship as his father before him had faced. From the beginning Charles played leading parts in big theatres, and he was paid considerably more than a starvation wage. After all, he had been given the name of Kean as well as a gentleman's education by his father.

Father and son were not permanently estranged. Edmund was incapable of bearing malice towards his own child, and though he had never wanted him to become an actor — he had wanted him to become something more fitted to a gentleman — he was now possessively proud of him. Charles, for his part, was not above profiting from his father's histrionic experience and advice. But he remained none the less his mother's child. He was a born prig. He would grow into a vain and pompous man. He was righteous and devout. He would lead a model life. He would earn and save money. He was persevering. He would become a leader of his profession and would have a good influence on the theatre. He would be honoured by a host of distinguished acquaintances. But he would never be lighted up by a spark of his father's genius.

His attitude to Edmund, even at the age of eighteen, was more parental than filial. He treated him as the brilliant black sheep of the family. It was out of loyalty to his mother that he refused to sleep under the same roof as Ophelia Benjamin. If he had been more loyal to his father, he might have done something more drastic. For Ophelia was hurting Edmund far more than she could ever hope to injure Mary. She was robbing

him of life itself. She was driving him to such feats of extravagance that he could not afford to rest for long. She was
digging her spurs into an old war horse, making him gallop
after gold who had not really the strength to walk.

The result was that after three months of rest in 1829, he
was back fulfilling provincial engagements that drained his
remaining strength still further. He was back in Bute in August
when he learned that Charles Kemble was faced with bankruptcy.
Edmund was one of the distinguished players who offered to
appear at Covent Garden without pay during the coming
season. He wrote from Bute to say that in spite of his precarious
health he would come to London and would give three gratuitous
performances.

But by the time he arrived the Covent Garden management
no longer had an urgent need of him. Charles Kemble was out
of danger, and was heading towards a new prosperity. He had
been saved from bankruptcy in a full-blooded, theatrical fashion
by his eighteen-year-old daughter, Fanny. She had made a
sensational debut as Juliet on 5th October, and was now the
idol of the town. Three times a week she was impersonating the
heroines of tragedy, and was drawing huge, excited, adoring
crowds to Covent Garden.

She was not, for several reasons, within measurable distance
of being a great actress. She had had no proper training; she was
unambitious and even out of love with her calling. On her own
admission, the theatre, 'from the preparations behind the scenes
to the representations before the curtain,' was repugnant to
her. 'My task seems so useless,' she wrote, 'that but for the very
useful pecuniary results, I think I would rather make shoes.'

And yet her triumph is easily explained. The mere announcement that Fanny Kemble — niece of Mrs Siddons and the great
John Philip — was coming from the nursery, as it were, to
rescue her harassed father from the threats of angry creditors
struck deep into the hearts of the British public. On the night
of 5th October she sat in her strange dressing room, surrounded
by anxious relatives, clutching her hands convulsively together
and weeping large, heavy tears which washed away her make-
up. But she need have had no fear. The battle was already won.

In front, a vast audience were waiting impatiently for her entrance. They cheered her wildly when she appeared at last, looking so fresh and innocent and timid. They went mad about her when they found that her voice was clear and that some of her mannerisms were reminiscent of Aunt Sarah.

It was not the time for dispassionate judgement. In many scenes Fanny Kemble was stilted and artificial and obviously 'taught'. But no one cared. She was irresistible. Next morning the critics, overcome by softer emotions, mistook Fanny Kemble's brave sweetness for genius.

Leigh Hunt, who saw her a few weeks later, was proof against her immature charms. 'We doubt not from that ingenuous face of hers,' he wrote in the *Tatler*, 'that she is a very nice girl and we think she has very cleverly seized what has been taught her. But we see nothing in her at present, that we should not expect to find in twenty others.'

Leigh Hunt was the first of the great critics. A quarter of a century earlier he had stood out alone against the Master Betty hysteria. But now as then he was a solitary exponent of reason. The Fanny Kemble boom was on.

And Edmund Kean was expected to bow to it. He wrote on 19th November to Bartley, the Covent Garden stage manager:

> I am very unwell . . . the fatigue of travelling such an immense distance, has nearly overcome me, & nothing but the *cause*, the *cause* my soul cou'd reconcile me to the exertion. Numerous engagements are pouring in upon me, & I shou'd like to get rid of the three nights as fast as I conveniently can — what say you to next Monday, Wednesday, Friday & give the management to understand that I play on no other nights but those I have been accustomed to in both London theatres.

He sent that letter as a challenge and he knew what answer to expect, for the stage has little sense of the courtesy that is owed to age and experience. He was duly informed by Bartley that Mondays, Wednesdays and Fridays were engaged for Miss Kemble's appearances. He would have to make his arrangements accordingly.

The implication was obvious, and Edmund could not tolerate it. Without deigning another word to Bartley, he entered into a new contract with Stephen Price.

The inevitable row followed. The old cry was taken up once again. Kean was petty and vain and jealous. In his unpardonable arrogance he had stooped to insulting the defenceless Fanny Kemble. But this time the furore in the newspapers failed to arouse the indignation of the public. Perhaps people realized that Edmund, in spite of his lack of magnanimity, had at least some right on his side. Magnanimity is a precious virtue, but it requires the strength and confidence of which Edmund was so sadly in need. He was tired and ill; he was still struggling to keep his position in the theatre against overwhelming odds; and before he had attained it he had already shown an infinite capacity for suffering. Was it not a little hard to expect him suddenly to play second fiddle to a prim and proper girl who had neither fought nor yet been hurt? When he reappeared at Drury Lane as Richard on 2nd December, he was given a grand reception by an audience who evidently believed that he deserved it.

Audiences were, in any case, beginning to treat him far more tolerantly than they once had. Even when he exasperated them, they tried to curb their anger. No doubt they understood that a man so lacerated as he could not bear the infliction of many more wounds. And he was, after all, a most treasured thing. They did not want him to die.

Throughout December and January he played at Drury Lane to packed houses. Sometimes he was apparently ill, and his performances were very disappointing. But, in front, they sat patiently, hoping against hope that his feebleness in the early scenes merely meant that he was 'husbanding his strength' for a terrific effort later on. They who had once consigned him to damnation were now satisfied by a few brief glimpses of his true genius.

His failures to rise above his physical weakness were becoming more frequent; and he was himself mortified by them. At the beginning of February he wrote to Dunn, the Drury Lane Treasurer: 'I am almost ashamed to ask for payment for so feeble a performance as my last Richard, nor would I but for Doctor's bills — for Lancets & Boluses — however I hope all will soon be better than ever, these little casualties of nature teach us to be cautious.'

And yet it was not only for money that he acted. 'The spark of ambition' still burned. While the doctors bled him and dosed him in order to keep life in his body, he was again attempting to learn a new part. He was going to impersonate Shakespeare's Henry V. Rehearsals at Drury Lane had already started, and the management was planning an elaborate, expensive production.

The announcement caused great excitement, and they were all there to see him on the night of 8th March, 1830: the critics, the connoisseurs and the eager throng in the pit. They were restive; for already the play had been once postponed at the last moment and now it was very late starting. Three times the orchestra had repeated the overture, but the curtain still remained obstinately down. Was Kean ill again? Or was he drunk? Or was he being coaxed on to the stage against his will?

He looked well enough when they saw him at last, dressed in a magnificently regal costume of purple and crimson and gold, seated on a throne, with his courtiers around him. But as soon as they had finished applauding him and were silent, he revealed himself as a mere dummy decked out as an actor. His very fineries added to his tragic absurdity. He did not know his words.

He spoke a few lines haltingly and waited for a prompt; then echoed the prompter's voice and stopped again. He floundered, gagged, cut, transposed and made his part quite meaningless and ineffective.

It was like *Ben Nazir* all over again, except that the play was by Shakespeare, not by Grattan. This time the audience could not doubt who was the real culprit. For two acts they endured the travesty, hoping in vain that Kean would recover his faculties — and then their patience snapped. The tumult and the shouting began.

Midway through the fifth act Edmund tried to quell the row by a humble appeal for mercy. He removed his royal hat and walked towards the footlights. 'I have worked hard, ladies and

gentlemen, for your amusement,' he said, 'but time and circumstances must plead my apology. I stand here in the most degraded
situation, and call upon you as my countrymen to show your
usual liberality.'

A few people cheered him. But the majority of the audience,
who had wasted their shillings, were for the moment too
annoyed and too disgusted to be moved by pity or sentiment.
They interrupted his speech brutally. 'Why do you get drunk?'
they yelled. They continued to hiss until the curtain came
down upon the first and last performance of Kean in *Henry V*.

When Edmund left the theatre that night he feared that his
career was smashed beyond hope of repair. The humiliation of
failure was bad enough in itself, but worse, far worse, was the
memory of those angry howls from the audience. Of course,
he would never again attempt to learn a new part. But would
the matter end there? Would he even be allowed to play his
famous characters in peace? He had been made to pay so heavy
a price for his sins in the past that he lived in terror now of the
public's vengeance. Perhaps, he would be booed on his next
appearance; and if so he would have to retire from the stage, for
he knew he could not face another persecution. He would
rather end his life as he had begun it — by picking up pennies
in barns and fairgrounds.

He sent an appeal to the *Times*:

... want of memory is not want of heart, and while a pul-
sation is left it beats with gratitude and affection to that
public which brought me from obscurity into a light I never
dreamt of, and it overpowered me. I find too late I must rest
on my former favours ... let me once more pursue that path
which led me to your favour, and die in grateful recollection
of the debt I owe to a sympathising though sometimes an
unjustly angry public.

At the same time he wrote to W.H. Halpin, editor of the *Star*:

Fight for me, I have no resources in myself; mind is gone,
and body is hopeless. God knows my heart. I would do, but

cannot. Memory, the first of goddesses, has forsaken me, and I am left without a hope but from those old resources that the public and myself are tired of. God damn ambition. The soul leaps, the body falls.

But the days when Edmund required an apologist were over. His own lamentable state was all the protection that he needed against excessive punishment. When he made his entrance as Richard on 15th March 'his frame was almost convulsed, and perspiration rolled down his cheeks'; but he never heard the hisses which he dreaded. Instead, the pit rose up and cheered him, and in the boxes they clapped condescendingly. He pulled himself together and gave one of his best performances. With the line 'Richard's himself again'* he brought the house down. The audience did not think that it was true, but they hoped that it might be. They were as much moved as he. He was their wayward lover, and, though they had often treated him heartlessly in the past, they clung to him desperately now, because they were in danger of losing him forever.

A few days later Edmund wrote almost buoyantly to Halpin, 'I am reinstated in all my dignities and privileges'. He meant, of course, that his worst fears had not been realized; and that, in his world of precarious values, he was at least secure in the knowledge that he would never have to go a begging for his bread.

But his relief, though great at first, was not a permanent cause for joy. From the beginning it had been his tragedy that he could not accept a limit to his achievements; and now, both as an artist and as a man, he rebelled hopelessly against his incapacities. His body ached and his mind was failing. But his 'soul leaped'. Ambition would not be God damned.

He knew it was impossible for him to learn a new part. He had finally settled for that. And yet he could not resign himself to the prospect of 'resting on his former favours'. In spite of his protests to the contrary, that was not his way; it never had been. His feelings were as intense, as impulsive, as emotional

*   From *Richard III* as altered by Colley Cibber.

as always. They fought against his ailments for expression. He submerged them with brandy, but they came to the surface again and drove him on. There must be something he could do which would be fresh and startling.

Since he was refused the lesseeship of Drury Lane after Stephen Price had resigned, he announced in June that he was going to close his professional career after a last grand and especially remunerative tour of the United States. From 16th June to 12th July he gave a series of farewell performances at the Haymarket, which were naturally well attended. On 19th July he moved a few doors down the road to the more spacious King's Theatre. There he gave what was supposed to be his final appearance before a London audience.

That night no one could have doubted his magnetism. An hour before the curtain went up every inch of space in the vast auditorium was filled by a huge crowd who had already experienced a surfeit of waiting in the sultry heat outside the closed doors of the playhouse. Those who had seats breathed foul air and listened to the angry shouts of men and the piercing shrieks of women. But they were fortunate even if they were uncomfortable. At least they were envied by others who stood, closely packed together, in the lobbies, on the stairs, in the orchestra pit and even in the wings of the stage itself.

Edmund fully exploited the drama of the occasion. He had specially engaged a glittering cast of actors to support him and to do him honour. He did not impersonate just one character, but appeared in scenes from five of his famous plays. He was first discovered dressed as Richard III and mounted high on a throne. He arose and bowed in acknowledgement of the applause that greeted him. Then he began to act his part.

For three hours and more he held his suffocated audience under his spell. He gave them something to remember of his Richard, his Shylock, his Othello, his Overreach and his Macbeth. They noticed that as time went on he became increasingly exhausted; that in Overreach he was feeble, and forgetful even in Macbeth. But they did not care. They grasped frantically at the points which were as fine as always, and merely regretted the lapses.

At the end there were scenes of wild enthusiasm. The stage was drowned in flowers, and the cheering thundered so long and so loudly that it was minutes before Edmund could speak. That was the moment for which he had been waiting, the great climax of his evening. 'Ladies and gentlemen,' he began, 'I hope that none of you can understand. . . the acute suffering I endure now that I am about to quit the country that gave me birth, and the people whom I have adored, to visit a land where perhaps nothing but ill-health and sorrow await me.' And he concluded after a good deal more of fustian. 'Ladies and Gentlemen, the time has now arrived for me to return you all my most fervent thanks, and to bid you a long, a last farewell.'

He bowed repeatedly and slowly disappeared from sight. The audience remained a little while, cheering an empty stage; and then, in their turn, left the theatre.

But it was all so much pathetic make-believe — the advertised intent, the carefully prepared speech, the sorrowful departure. How could Edmund, who had saved nothing from his huge earnings — about half a million pounds a year in today's money — ever hope to retire? And how could he, who scarcely had the strength to walk across the stage, brave the risk of a further adventure on the other side of the Atlantic Ocean?

Perhaps in his passion to test the heart of the British public he had deceived himself. Perhaps he really did believe that he would go to America, that he would accumulate a vast fortune there — vast enough to satisfy the demands of his rapacious mistress — and would eventually return to his own country rich and independent. But the events of the next few months served to awaken him from his dream. They proved to him that in the United States he might meet not merely 'sorrow and ill-fortune' but death. He was afraid to die in a foreign land where he would be far away from those few who were still dear to him.

He spent the summer, according to plan, 'bidding good-bye' to his provincial audiences. He played in Brighton, Liverpool, Norwich, Yarmouth, Cheltenham, Peterborough and Manchester. But his tour was hardly triumphant. It was interrupted by frequent bouts of illness. In Manchester, according to the *Theatrical Observer*, 'he had a most dreadful attack of "prurulent opthalmia." ' He dared not entrust his case to a local physician, so he sent for Mr Douchez, one of his London doctors. Douchez found him 'acting Richard so blind as not to be able to distinguish Lady Anne from his "Cousin of Buckingham" except by "their sweet voices". ' And this was the gallant warrior who had wanted to enslave the American public once more.

In October he went to Bute for a short rest. He did not guess then that he was spending his last holiday in his island paradise, but he must have known that he would never be able to live there in retirement. His idea of a farewell visit to the United States had already receded beyond the bounds of possibility; and now he was no longer certain that he even wished to retire. He was so lonely that there was no joy in his heart and very little will to be alive except that which is induced by fear of the unknown. Ophelia had deprived him of friends and of the money with which he should have purchased peace. Now she, in her turn, had deserted him. He hated her with the hatred of an ill-used lover, yet still desired her. To her he attributed his misery, yet was miserable without her. He felt that if he did not go on working he would fall down dead. But he could not work without the aid of those artificial stimulants which were eating away the least vestiges of his strength.

The newspapers, of course, could not resist printing some jibes at his expense about all the meaningless fuss that had attended his farewell performance. But the public were delighted to have him back again. Leigh Hunt, who reviewed his Richard in the *Tatler*, stated that he was infinitely the greatest actor 'he ever saw' and that he was as far ahead of Macready as Macready was superior to the rest of the contemporary tragedians. Of course, there were times when he grasped his sceptre with less firmness than of old. In the tent scene, for instance, when he started up from his horrid dream, he made such a feeble business of the rush forward (or coming rather) that the house seemed inclined to be angry with it.

But how fine he is, when he is fine! [wrote Leigh Hunt] How true! how full of gusto! how intense! What perfect amalgamation there is of the most thorough feeling and the most graceful idealism! The first four lines which Richard utters on coming on: *Now is the winter of our discontent*, etc. were as beautifully delivered as they could ever have been, especially the last:

And all the clouds that lower'd upon our house
In the deep bosom of the Ocean buried.

Kean in speaking that last line, held forth his arm and in a beautiful style of deliberate triumph, uttering his words with inward majesty, pointed his finger downwards; as if he saw the very ocean beneath him from some promontory and beheld it close over the past.

'We could not help persuading ourselves,' Leigh Hunt added, 'that Mr Kean might recover all that he wanted. There is nothing in his time of life to prevent it.'

Edmund was, in fact, forty-two years old. But there were many sad reasons why he could not retrieve the past. Leigh Hunt hit on what was perhaps the most important of them a few months later. He noticed that while playgoers in the pit applauded Kean unstintingly, the people in the boxes seemed loath to display even the mildest enthusiasm. They behaved as if they had been dragged to the theatre against their will — by some magnetic power which in spite of themselves they could not resist. Leigh Hunt sensed that Edmund was hurt by their attitude and so he took the opportunity to address them as follows:

Do at least justice to your own discernment, be at the trouble of applauding what you think worth going to see, and let not the town-talk with which a man of genius has been mixed, and with which his genius has nothing to do, induce you to sit as if you were afraid to applaud him, and had no business where you are.

But in truth Society *was* ashamed to be pleased by Edmund's acting. Though nothing could alter the fact that he was a great tragedian, no words, however ably or reasonably expressed, could change Society's attitude towards the man.

4

Though Edmund realized that he would never be able to retire to Bute, he wanted none the less to have some kind of permanency in his life. So when he learned that the King's Theatre, Richmond Green, was in the market, he at once offered to rent it. He had always fancied himself as an actor-manager, and now it would suit him perfectly to be in control of a small country playhouse, not too far away from London. He wrote to Mr Budd, the agent, on 10th February, 1831:

> ... the fact is I am weary of scampering about His Majesty's domains, and till I make my final bow to the public, I think a good company, well appointed and governed by a man of forty years' theatrical experience, would fix upon my retreat both pleasure and profit. If you would do me the favour to let me know if my name would not be objectionable to the proprietor, or my industry to the public, the rent, taxes, etc., etc., you will confer an obligation on Yours truly, Edmund Kean.

Before the spring of 1831, Edmund had become lessee of the King's Theatre, and had taken up his residence in the picturesque cottage that adjoined it. It was not altogether a sensible move on his part, for he soon discovered that far from enabling him to live in comfortable seclusion, as he had hoped, it forced him into a veritable orgy of exertion.

He appeared often on his own stage during the following year, but he appeared on many other stages besides in order to pay for his theatre's losses. Indeed, his professional commitments were so arduous and so varied — he appeared in London, Bristol, Dublin, Edinburgh and so on up and down the United Kingdom — that they would have exhausted an actor in perfect health. As it was, though it is no wonder his progress was often arrested by illness, he was killing himself as much by overwork as by brandy.

Samuel Phelps, one of the best known of Victorian actors, was at this time a very young member of the company in York, and was cast as Tubal to Edmund's Shylock. Edmund didn't bother to attend rehearsal, and though Phelps had been put through his paces by John Lee, he was a trifle puzzled at the actual performance, for Edmund 'prowled about the stage like a caged tiger'. However, he did his best. 'He dodged him up and down, and crossed when he·crossed.' Everything seemed to be going smoothly when Edmund hissed into his ear: 'Get out of my focus — blast you — get out of my focus.' Phelps looked into the wings, where John Lee was standing. Lee motioned him to stand higher up. He had committed the unpardonable sin of blocking the float's light from shining into Edmund's face.

After the play was over he was summoned to Edmund's dressing room. He found him drinking copiously of brandy with Bill Anderton, a provincial actor, whom Edmund had known and liked in his strolling player days. Edmund welcomed Phelps; 'Have a glass of grog young stick-in-the mud. You'll be an actor one of these days, sir; but mind, the next time you play with me, for God's sake steer clear of my focus.'

One gets from that a sharp picture of the vulgarian Edmund Kean. And one is given a similar impression from a letter written to John Lee on 10th April, 1831.

Dear Lee,
   What day do I open in Cheltenham. The stupid son of a bitch has not dated his letter, write me Birmingham. Get as much money as you can and save it for me. I shall send you money as soon as I get it [illegible]. I won't say I wish her dead but I'll be damned if I don't. Yours truly, Edmund Kean.

To this, he added a playful little postscript; 'Tiddy no sausages out of season capitol (sic) cigars and grog.'
'Tiddy' was Miss Tidswell who had come to look after Edmund, and, to judge from the postscript, she seems to have had as little control over him as she had in his childhood.

Whether or not the last sentence in the letter refers to Ophelia, there is no doubt that Edmund's 'last will' in which she features prominently was written at Richmond. It begins: 'The villainy of the Irish Strumpet Ophelia Benjamin, has undone me and though I despise her, I feel life totally valueless without her. I leave her my curses.'

Another famous figure of the Victorian theatre, Helen Faucit, formed an impression of the Edmund Kean who loved children and was a child himself. Helen Faucit was still a school-girl when she met him, and she used to spend her holidays with her sister, who lived at Richmond.

> One of my earliest and vivid recollections [she wrote] was a meeting with 'the great Edmund Kean', as my sister called him. He was her pet hero. She had seen him act, and through friends had a slight acquaintance with him. Wishing her little 'birdie', as she often called me to share all her pleasures, she often took me with her to the green for the chance of seeing him as he strolled there with his aunt old Miss Tidswell. The great man had been very ill, so that all our expectations had been frequently disappointed. At last about noon one very warm sunny day my sister's eager eye saw the two figures in the far distance ... As we drew nearer I would gladly have run away. I was startled, frightened at what I saw — a small, pale man with a fur cap and wrapped in a fur coat. He looked to me as if come from the grave. A stray lock of very dark hair crossed his forehead, under which shone eyes which looked dark, and yet bright as lamps. So large were they, so piercing, so absorbing, I could see no other features. I shrank from them behind my sister, but she whispered to me that it would be unkind to show any fear, so we approached and were kindly greeted by the pair.
>
> Oh, what a voice was that which spoke! It seemed to come from far away — a long, long way behind him. After the first salutation, it said, 'Who is this little one?' When my sister had explained, the face smiled (I was reassured by the smile, and the face looked less terrible), and he asked me where I went to school, and which books I liked best. Alas! I could

not then remember that I liked any, but my ever good angel sister said she knew I was fond of poetry, for I had just won a prize for recitation. Upon this the face looked still more kindly on me, and we all moved together to a seat under the trees. Then the far-away hollow voice — but it was not harsh — spoke again, as he put his hand in mine, and bade me tell him whether I liked my school walks better than the walks at Richmond. This was too much, and it broke the ice of my silence. No indeed, Greenwich Park was very pretty . . . but Richmond! Nothing could be more beautiful! . . . My tongue ran on and on, and had after a time to be stopped, for my sister and the old lady thought I should fatigue the invalid. But he would not part just yet. He asked my name, and when it was told exclaimed, 'Oh, the old ballad — do you know it? which begins:

O, my Helen
There is to tellin'
Why love I fell in:
The grave, my dwellin'
Would I were well in!

I know now why with my Helen love I fell in; it is because she loves poetry and she loves Richmond. Will my Helen come and repeat her poetry for me some day?' This alarming suggestion at once silenced my prattle, and my sister had to express for me the honour and pleasure I felt. Here the interview ended; the kind hand was withdrawn which had lain in mine so heavily, and yet looked so thin and small. I did not know then how great is the weight of weakness. It was put upon my head, and I was bid Godspeed! I was to be sent for some day soon. But the day never came; the school days were at hand. Those wondrous eyes I never saw, and that distant voice I never heard again.

By the summer of 1832, Edmund's strength was gradually ebbing away. As the months went by, his appearances on the stage grew less frequent, for there was a limit to the revivifying powers of brandy. During periods of enforced idleness, his energy, lust, ambition were all frustrated, and he was thrown back on himself. He became the prisoner of his remorse, and was face to face with the awful realization that his tragedy was of his own making:

> This is the hour, when sluggards are in sleep
> That genius soars the air, or scours the deep
> Brings to the vision, all the days gone by,
> This heart, the good and ill which in it lie
> Looks on proud man, but as a worldly thing,
> Scarcely a shade twixt Beggar and a King,
> Whipt in his childhood, in manhood trained
> In all the vices which the fallen strained.

Those were lines that he penned when he had nothing else to do but contemplate his melancholy. He hated his thoughts, yet could not escape them. Sometimes he tried to lull himself into forgetfulness by playing the piano and listening to the sound of his own voice. Dr Smith, a local physician who attended him when he was at Richmond, remembered one such occasion. It was on a summer's evening in 1832:

> I crossed the green and went into the house, the door being open. In the twilight I saw the figure of Mr Lee, not very clearly defined, standing at the door of Mr Kean's sitting-room. The secretary, who was attentively listening to something, raised his finger to enjoin silence. The tragedian was sitting at the piano, accompanying himself to an inexpressibly beautiful singing of 'Those Evening Bells'. Next he sang with exquisite sweetness and pathos one or two of Moore's melodies, after which he repeated 'Those Evening Bells'. At first, he sang with great clearness, but gradually his voice became plaintive in the extreme, then tremulous then thick, as if with emotion. It slowly died, and a dead silence followed. I softly opened the door and went in. His head was bowed upon the piano, and as he raised it on hearing my approach a moonbeam fell upon the keys of the instrument, showing me that they were wet with tears.

He had abandoned hope of recovery. And now that he felt himself to be so close to death he was tormented less by his plight than by his awareness of its causes. He was in dread of some mysterious Divinity whom he did not understand but in whose existence he believed instinctively. Would his departure from this world mean the finish of his sufferings? Or would he have to pay further for his sins in an after-life? He wanted desperately to make atonement before it was too late. He was afraid to die while he was still at war with his own conscience or with God. At the end of his 'last will' he wrote the words 'forgive me oh Lord and receive my soul with mercy.'

His mother wrote to him in September of 1832 to say that she was very ill and to ask him for money in advance of her allowance. 'I am in a strange state of health,' she concluded, 'two days before I saw Harry everyone thought I could not live the night through, I am sorry that I live to trouble my dear child, and yet I cannot wish to die. *Let me see you!*'

It was not the first time she had appealed to his charity in this way. The Harry she referred to in her letter was his half-brother, another bastard son of hers, and he was already keeping him and his offspring. None the less Ann Carey asked to come to stay in his house at Richmond, and a few days after her arrival Aunt Tid left, because, one supposes, she resented the intrusion. It was a kind of re-run of his childhood, and the exchange could not have been for the better. For Ann Carey was an incurable invalid, and quite incapable of nursing her son. She spent most of her time in bed. According to Dr Smith, 'she proved to be a low, dissipated, illiterate woman'.

In December, Edmund's penitence became transparent. He wrote to his wife:

Dear Mary, Let us be no longer fools. Come home, forget and forgive. If I have erred, it was my head, not my heart, and most severely have I suffered for it. My future life shall be employed in contributing to your happiness, and you, I trust, will return that feeling by a total obliteration of the past. Your wild but really affectionate husband, Edmund Kean.

But Mary did not reciprocate his sentiments. In her heart there was no desire for a reconciliation with the man who she supposed had wronged her grievously. Two years before she might have gone back to him, if he had asked her. But now her future was secure with Charles, who was doing very well for himself. True, to please her son, she did visit Edmund once or twice near the end. But one cannot imagine that she brought him much comfort. She had nothing to offer him — neither affection nor even pity. Only a few months after his death she would be accused, in *Fraser's Magazine* of 'compendiously collecting his vices for the contempt or execration of the world'. One knows from her letters to Barry Cornwall that she never learned to respect his memory.

Meanwhile Edmund was finding it increasingly difficult to pay for mere existence. Though his responsibilities were as onerous as ever, his earnings in the past few months had dropped alarmingly, and he had no savings. His health was now so precarious that he could never be certain of living through a part. Every time he appeared on the stage he gambled with mortality. There is a pathetic story of his physical weakness — typical of many others — which was told by Johnston, the actor, who once played Tubal to his Shylock. At the end of the scene, Edmund was too exhausted to make his exit without assistance, and so he changed the line, 'Go, Tubal, and meet me at our synagogue' to 'Lead me to our synagogue'. Then, using Johnston for support, he dragged himself into the wings.

But it was a choice for him between courting death and starving to death. He could not afford idleness so long as he had the power to move. During November and December (1832) he gave no fewer than fourteen performances at Drury Lane; eight of them were as Othello to the Iago of William Charles Macready, whom he had finally been forced to meet. It proved an uncomfortable battle, though it drew the town. Macready, smug, self centred, snobbish, superior, had no sympathy for Edmund. He was proud to hold the conventional view of him — that he was a great tragedian who had sacrificed his talents to his vices. He disliked the experience of appearing on the same stage with him. He called him that 'low man'. In his diary of 10th December he wrote, 'Acted well when Kean did not interfere with me.'

Edmund, for his part, still regarded Macready as a dreaded rival. Even now he could not bear the thought of being eclipsed by him. He struggled against his ailments to dominate the scene. And by fair means or foul he succeeded at least in holding his own. G.H. Lewes, who as a very young man saw one of these performances of *Othello*, remembered how puny Kean appeared beside Macready, until the third act, when roused by Iago's taunts and insinuations, he moved towards him with a gouty hobble, seized him by the throat and in a well-known explosion, 'Villain! be sure thou prove', etc., seemed to swell into a stature which made Macready appear small. 'On that evening, when gout made it difficult for him to display his accustomed grace . . . such was the irresistible pathos — manly not tearful — which vibrated in his tones and expressed itself in look and gestures that old men leaned their heads upon their arms and fairly sobbed.'

On 19th February (1833) Edmund fainted during a performance of Sir Giles Overreach at Brighton, and had to be carried from the stage. 'I fear it will be my last dying speech,' he said afterwards.

It wasn't — not quite. He rallied again, and again understood how urgently he was in need of money. He asked Captain Polhill, who had succeeded Alexander Lee as lessee of Drury Lane, to make him a loan to £500 on account of his future performances. Captain Polhill declined. The services of an actor who might fade out at any moment were not sufficient security.

Edmund was as sensitive as ever to insult. To have been refused a trifling favour by the theatre that he had once rescued from bankruptcy was an affront not to be borne. Impulsively, he sent a medical certificate to Drury Lane, and signed a new contract with Covent Garden from where the Kembles had recently departed for a tour of the United States.

On Monday, 25th March, he was billed to play Othello to the Iago of his son Charles. Naturally, the announcement caused a sensation for the two Keans had never been seen together in

London. 'It is mere quackery,' Macready wrote in his diary. But it drew a large, excited and sentimental house.

When Edmund arrived at the theatre he looked very pale, and he was shivering. It was only after he had swallowed many glasses of brandy and had listened to the encouraging words of the theatre officials, who hovered anxiously about him, that he decided that he had enough strength to act at all.

He was rewarded with a storm of cheering on his entrance. It was a grand, dramatic moment for which the audience had been waiting impatiently. Edmund bowed again and again. Then he took Charles by the hand and led him towards the footlights. He presented his heir to the public. The house broke into a renewed frenzy of applause. Edmund could not repress his tears.

He struggled feebly through the first two acts. He was not pleased with himself, but he was proud of his son. He remarked to someone in the wings, 'Charles is getting on tonight, he's acting very well. I suppose that is because he's acting with me.'

The third act began. He had warned Charles: 'Mind that you keep before me. Don't get behind me in this act. I don't know that I shall be able to kneel; but if I do be sure you lift me up.'

He reached the line 'Othello's occupation's gone', the line which heralded his terrific explosion, 'Villain, be sure thou prove my love a whore,' with which he'd dwarfed Booth and Young and Macready and all the other Iagos who had ever crossed his path. But now the anticipated onslaught never came. Edmund was on the point of collapse. He had lost the power of speech. A deep mist was blotting out his vision and a racking pain was paralysing his limbs. He flung his arms round Charles. 'Oh God, I am dying,' he whispered through agonized lips, 'Speak to them for me,' and then he lost consciousness.

He was carried from the stage and later to a neighbouring tavern, where he was put to bed and attended by his London physician, Dr Carpue.

Meanwhile at Covent Garden, the audience had not waited to see *Othello* concluded with another actor in the name part. Instinctively, they had known, perhaps, that though Edmund was not yet dead, a great and tragic epoch in the theatre had reached its close.

5

He knew that he had played his last part.

Back at Richmond he was tended by James Smith and by his medical advisers from London — Douchez and Carpue. He did nothing to rebuild his strength. He refused to eat food, except when it was administered to him in the form of medicine. He continued to sustain himself on brandy. It was only his will that kept him alive.

Perhaps, he fought for the chance to say goodbye to Aunt Tid. She would not come to him now that Ann Carey was at Richmond. One day towards the end of April he drove to her lodgings at 4 Camera Street, Chelsea.

The journey imposed too great a strain on his physique. When he returned home that evening he said that he had 'caught his death blow', and called for brandy, which made him feel no better.

On 1st May his doctors realized that there was no hope. On 2nd May Charles and Mary came to take their leave of him. Yet he lingered on for another fortnight. He had done with the world. But his life ebbed painfully away. It seemed to have shrunk and to have become encompassed within the walls of his own room at Richmond. There, on his bed, were piled the classical volumes that he had never found the time to read and now had not the strength to open; there sitting round the bed were a few devoted friends to whom he recited Shakespeare and talked of his triumphs and his failures; and there, within his reach, was a supply of brandy which was killing him, but without which he could not survive.

On 14th May he sank into unconsciousness. Throughout the night his secretary, John Lee, and his surgeon, George Douchez, watched over him. In the early morning of 15th May he opened his eyes and seemed to recognize them. But he could not speak. He died a few hours later.

In Richmond as in no other part of the United Kingdom, Edmund Kean was beloved. He was the most celebrated trage- dian of the century, and if the inhabitants had known him simply as that, he might have been stared at but he would not have been revered. He won their respect, because for the first time in his life he acquired despite all his weaknesses, with which they were doubtless familiar, a definite if pathetic dignity. It may have been a dignity that he could not avoid. He was physically unable to make a habit of drinking himself silly publicly at the Castle Inn or one of the other local taverns. They saw him only when he went for walks on the green or when he climbed the hill to gaze at the view from the terrace, a venerable figure, wrapped up, even on the warmest days of summer, in a capa- cious fur cloak. He had become, as it were, a part of the life of Richmond, so that now that he was dead, his fellow inhabitants were saddened by the loss of a beloved neighbour and hastened to pay honour to the shade of a distinguished townsman. They crowded to pass, in silence, by his coffin while it lay at Mr Piggott's the undertaker. They were anxious even to spend their money on raising a memorial to him and would have done so had not Charles claimed that right as his own.

In the rest of the country the loss of Edmund Kean, the *actor*, was mourned. For he had become, despite his young age, an institution: a decayed, battered, perhaps a discreditable institution, but an institution nevertheless, and one which people did not wish to be deprived of. Now that he was gone it seemed — to use his own lofty phrase — as if the last great 'representative of Shakespeare's heroes' had been taken away from them. But the passing of Kean, the man, was little cause for regret. Apart from a few far-sighted intellectuals ready to excuse his weaknesses and a few loud-throated vulgarians eager to eulogize his excesses, the public parted from him without sorrow.

Admittedly, there was pomp and ceremony enough on the day of his funeral. Macready was one of the pall-bearers. But Macready had only been brought to Richmond by his chronic fear of public opinion. This reluctance to honour a departed colleague was not prompted by professional jealousy. Macready had often admitted his admiration of Kean the actor, but for Kean the man he had nothing but supreme contempt. A year later, he was to record for posterity that 'Kean was the greatest disgrace to the art of acting of all the disgraceful members that ever practised it.'

The old Parish Church was, indeed, crowded for the funeral of Edmund Kean on 25th May, 1833. But if one excepts his few devoted friends such as John Lee and Sheridan Knowles, only the inhabitants of Richmond who sat silently at the back, saved all the outward show of grief from empty mockery. They, in truth, were sorrowfully conscious of the solemnity of the occasion. They shared the emotional feelings of the parson, the Rev Mr Campbell, as he read the burial service. They believed it rightly proclaimed:

His body is buried in Peace
But his name shall live for evermore.

Appendix

Appendix

The first of the six biographies of Edmund Kean was published two years after his death and appears to have been largely based on information that the author (Barry Cornwall) received from Mary Kean. By no means all of this is reliable.

Harold Hillebrand, who published his very scholarly life of Kean in 1933 and corrected many of the errors made by previous biographers, appears none the less to have agreed with Cornwall in his assessment of Mary's character. I was the first of the biographers to disagree, and my disagreement was based not only on a study of her letters to Cornwall but on her correspondence with Henry Sigell, Kean's solicitor.

Though I did get hold of a certain amount of primary source material, which was not available to Hillebrand, I disagreed with him in only one other important respect, and that was over his interpretation of Kean's last will to mean that Ophelia stayed with him to the end. The opposite interpretation is *prima facie* just as likely and must, I think, be true, for no one ever remarked seeing Ophelia at Richmond, and no mention of her is made in any letters while Kean lived there. Moreover, it is inconceivable that Aunt Tid would have agreed to sleep under the same roof as the woman who had alienated most of Kean's friends. According to one account — unsubstantiated — Ophelia left Kean for a husband and settled in Frith Street, Soho.

Mr FitzSimons inclines to accept my view of Mary, rather than Hillebrand's. Mary died, incidentally, in her house at Kleydell, near Horndean (Hampshire) on 13th March, 1849. The house had been given her by Charles.

Mr FitzSimons also says that Aunt Tid 'chased Ophelia from the house' (at Richmond). I do not know whether he has found a separate source for this or whether he is relying on supposition. As I have said, he does not appear to have had any sources that Hillebrand and I did not have other than Winston's diaries.

In the use of these diaries, I have relied exclusively on the publication of selections from them edited by Alfred L. Nelson and Gilbert B. Cross and published by the Society for Theatre Research in 1974.

The selections, which include virtually all that concern Edmund Kean, are mostly taken from a manuscript at present in the possession of the Henry E. Huntington Library in California. However, the initial entries that the editors have used, covering the Drury Lane period from 1819 to 1820, come from a manuscript belonging to the Garrick Club, whose first secretary was James Winston.

In the extracts that I have quoted directly, I have followed the editors in their use of square brackets, though I have not bothered to indicate, as they do, the few names or passages which the diarist enciphered. They employ square brackets to supply words omitted, to add information about authors, titles and dates, and to give synopses of relevant material too lengthy to be quoted in full. They also put a question mark in square brackets followed by a word to indicate their uncertainty about whether their reading of the word is correct, and place words inside the brackets to indicate a doubtful editorial addition.

There is one small fact that emerges from the diaries which FitzSimons seems to have missed. Hillebrand states that Kean used Lee as a replacement for Phillips as his secretary, and FitzSimons accepts this. Yet it is clear from entries in the diaries of 6th February and 12th February, 1827, that Lee was already his secretary before Kean lost the services of Phillips.

FitzSimons is the only one of the biographers to furnish a full bibliography. I have not done the same, since this would be mostly a matter of duplication, but instead have relied on occasional footnotes where these seemed necessary. In the appendix to my original biography I wrote: 'I have neither quoted sources which are obvious from the text itself nor have I bothered to prove details which have already been proved. I have confined my attention to new matters which may arouse controversy'.

Such matters were largely dependent on a number of letters and other documents, notably those in the possession of Ifan Kyrle Fletcher, which have long since been scattered. The only ones which may still be presumed to be where they were are the family paper which I discovered in the strong room of Charles Kean's solicitors and which included the letter from J.H. Merivale to Dr Drury.

Similarly, I made acknowledgements to people who are now, without exception, deceased. However I would wish to thank for the present book Dr G.N. Weber for his invaluable advice and Mrs Denys Howsley-Ward who typed, without complaint, my almost illegible manuscript.

Index